FALLING
IN LOVE WITH
PRAYER

FALLING
IN LOVE WITH
PRAYER

MIKE MACINTOSH

Victor®

The Bible Teacher's Teacher

COOK COMMUNICATIONS MINISTRIES
Colorado Springs, Colorado • Paris, Ontario
KINGSWAY COMMUNICATIONS LTD
Eastbourne, England

Victor® is an imprint of Cook Communications Ministries,
Colorado Springs, CO 80918
Cook Communications, Paris, Ontario
Kingsway Communications, Eastbourne, England

FALLING IN LOVE WITH PRAYER
© 2004 by Mike MacIntosh

Cover Design, Greg Jackson/JacksonDesignCo.llc
© Photo by Donna Day / Photodisc

First Paperback Printing, 2005
Printed in the United States of America
1 2 3 4 5 6 7 8 9 10 Printing/Year 08 07 06 05

ISBN 0-7814-4277-X (pbk.)

To my dear mother, Ruth Lane Osborn,
who at ninety years of age is still praying
and whose prayers keep me moving forward
in the battle for men's souls

CONTENTS

ACKNOWLEDGMENTS

My hero is my pastor. Chuck Smith taught me not only to pray but to pray believing.

He taught me the value of prayer and the power of prayer. He instructed me to pray from the Bible and from watching his own prayer life. As a young Christian man I attended every Saturday night prayer meeting that Chuck held for the men of his church. It was there that I knew I wanted to be a man of prayer.

Without George Mueller, Ries Howells, Andrew Murrary, Robert Murray McCheyne, Charles Spurgeon, Robert Evans, D. L. Moody, Dr. David Livingstone, and President Abraham Lincoln, I do not think I could have seen God using men through prayer in a meaningful way.

I thank God for Sandy, who has never stopped praying for me. And it is her prayers that capture my imagination the most.

Thanks to David Mehlis and his wonderful staff at Cook Communications who have all loved me and accepted me into their family. I acknowledge that I am not a writer, but I love the idea that my past thirty-four years with Jesus can be expressed in my latter years through the power of the written word. So to the Cook family—sales, editorial, and management—I thank you from the bottom of my heart.

Thanks to Keith Wall, who has done a fine job editing and helping me learn the craft.

My secretary, Renae, is one of the most wonderful resources God has given me.

Thanks to the wonderful people that, next to my family, I pray for the most—Horizon Christian Fellowship.

—MIKE MACINTOSH

ENRICH YOUR PRAYER EXPERIENCE

Christians have been given the incredible privilege of direct access to the heavenly Father.

Think of it: The Creator of the universe has invited us to talk with him day or night—any time, anywhere, and about anything. From our simplest petitions to our highest praises, God wants to hear from us. If we're thinking through a tough situation, he's there to give wisdom. If we're frightened, he's there to calm and encourage. Yet any of us can become so caught up in the busyness of life that we fail to take full advantage of this unparalleled honor. From talking with thousands of people each year in my ministry, I know for a fact that many—if not most—of my fellow Christians do not feel that they are experiencing a dynamic prayer life.

That's why I appreciate this new book, *Falling in Love with Prayer*, by my friend Mike MacIntosh. Mike is a living example of the power and privilege of prayer, a walking testament to God's amazing grace. Mike's early adulthood was spent in a wandering search for meaning, but after he trusted Jesus Christ as his Savior and Lord, God used him to launch what would become one of Southern California's most dynamic church ministries.

Key to Mike's success is his conviction that every Christian can and should enjoy an adventurous prayer life. In these pages he'll show you that when you fall in love with prayer, you fall in love with God. "If you have been remote and distant from God," Mike reminds us, "the Lord would like you to break the silence. He wants you to establish communication with him once again. ... He wants you to start living. When you go before the Lord in prayer, you bask in his radiant glory and beauty, and you experience the abundant life he has promised to all those who come to him in faith."

Over the years, many people have asked my father, Billy Graham, to what he attributes the impact of his worldwide ministry. His answer: "Pray unceasingly." Because I know the man quite well, I can verify that my father and mother have indeed lived by this credo. It was their unceasing prayer and unconditional love that steadied my faith during my own youthful rebellion; it was their prayer *and mine* that undergirded me as I launched the Samaritan's Purse ministry and, later, as I began my work with the Billy Graham Evangelistic Association. I am resolved to continue my father's legacy of unceasing prayer. I never want to be so busy that I inadvertently neglect the opportunity to praise and thank God and to give every care to him. No matter where you are in your spiritual journey, Mike MacIntosh's encouragement and guidance will help you enrich your prayer experience. Whether you need wisdom for life's constant challenges or want to rekindle your love affair

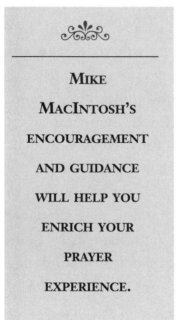

MIKE MACINTOSH'S ENCOURAGEMENT AND GUIDANCE WILL HELP YOU ENRICH YOUR PRAYER EXPERIENCE.

with God, this book is for you! I am confident that *Falling in Love with Prayer* will stimulate and motivate you to a more meaningful, adventurous prayer life.

—FRANKLIN GRAHAM

PRAYER: THE GRAND ADVENTURE

Most people would agree that prayer is a central component, an essential practice, of the Christian faith. But here is something about prayer that may surprise you: The majority of those people who affirm the importance of prayer have a complete misunderstanding of what it is all about. Indeed, I am convinced that if a questionnaire were circulated asking people to identify the meaning and purpose of prayer, most respondents would not be able to do so adequately.

Prayer is one of the wonderful gifts that God, the Creator of heaven and earth, has given to human beings. Prayer arrives at its destination faster than a letter gets to its recipient. It is, indeed, faster than sending an email to a friend or family member. It instantly connects the person praying to God without rerouting through exchanges, middlemen, or 10-10 numbers for long-distance phone calls.

But speed and efficiency are the least of prayer's beneficial attributes. When we understand prayer for what it is, we easily recognize it as an effective communication tool. Prayer, when used correctly, is so powerful that any human being living on planet earth can by faith make instant contact with the one who made him or her. It is not only an effective means for human beings to communicate with God, it is also an effective means for God to speak with human beings.

Isn't it interesting that it is *our* choice whether to establish that link between us and God, and between God and us? We can decide to speak with God and hear from him or to reject any dialogue with him.

Regaining the Sense of Excitement

When I was growing up, my brother and I had countless adventures together. Though we were only thirteen months apart in age, I still looked up to him as my "big brother." We grew up in Portland, Oregon, under the overcast, drizzly canopy so characteristic of that area. When the sun did poke through the clouds, a celebration seemed to break out all over the region.

The weather, however, had little effect on our plans. Rain or sun, we would be in "the woods" as we called them. Today, if you were to drive to the corner of 92nd and S. E. Taylor Streets, you would see several beautiful, manicured, park-like acres with a dozen or so fifty-foot-tall trees. But when we were growing up there, the place was overgrown and unkempt—quite a place for kids intent on building forts and hideaways. All the boys in the neighborhood would play army and hide-and-seek, among a myriad of other spirited games.

At the end of the day, we would all return home for dinner. Usually someone in the crowd would be sporting a new black eye or one of those nasty bruises that always seem to appear on young boys as naturally as pimples on a teenager. Indeed, as I ponder my growing-up years, they seem like a continual series of adventures, contests, and sometimes reckless antics.

Like me, you may look back on your childhood and adolescence as a time of excitement, fun, and endless anticipation of what might happen next. For most of us, though, the adventurous times of our lives begin to fade when we finish school and start to establish families and build careers. Eventually we all "settle down." Soon we find that a sense of monotony, predictability, and repetition has begun to creep into many aspects of our lives, including our spiritual lives. Prayer becomes a religious activity, a ritual, something that only old folks enjoy doing because they probably don't have anything else to do. Or so we rationalize.

Nothing could be further from the truth. Prayer can be—and should be—one of the most exhilarating experiences you and I could ever have. Our prayer life can become so energized and so passionate that our lives are pervaded by an edge-of-our-seat anticipation to see how God will respond next.

Three Simple Words

My desire is to open your eyes, your ears, and your heart to heaven. This is not necessarily a "how-to" book. Its purpose is to introduce you to biblical concepts of an adventurous prayer life. It is not a religious or theological treatise, but a book designed to be practical, helpful, and inspirational. Hopefully, it will also be fun to read, because it will help you grow as a person and as a Christian.

My premise is simple: If you fall in love with prayer, you cannot help but fall in love with God. The most wonderful thing I have enjoyed in more than thirty years of serving God is the understanding of onc of the Bible's most basic and profound principles: God is love. That understanding should take some of the mystery out of the spiritual world for you as it did for me. Those three simple words—God is love—open a vista for many people that they have never seen before.

> IF YOU FALL IN LOVE WITH PRAYER, YOU CANNOT HELP BUT FALL IN LOVE WITH GOD.

I pray that you will gain insight into the Bible's point of view on prayer while reading this presentation. I also pray that the stories of real people praying will deepen your understanding of God and communication with him even more.

We all need love, and since God is love (see 1 John 4:8), what better way to receive more love than from God himself. He is not hurried and overbooked. He waits with open ears and arms to hear your petitions, your requests, your heartaches, your failures, and your triumphs. He wants to hear you confess your sins so that he can forgive you of them and cleanse you of all unrighteousness (see 1 John 1:9).

So let's get started. Let's learn of God's design for prayer and his means of communicating with his children. It shouldn't take too many pages of reading before you start hearing the Holy Spirit speak to your heart and soul. And before you know it, this adventure called prayer will be so much fun and so thrilling that you will be praying alone and with people everywhere.

—MIKE MACINTOSH

CHAPTER ONE

THE INCREDIBLE PRIVILEGE OF PRAYER

"Real prayer comes not from gritting our teeth, but from falling in love."
RICHARD FOSTER

If you fall in love with prayer, you will fall in love with God. That is the theme woven throughout this book. But how do you fall in love with prayer? Many people pray very little—or not at all—because they think of prayer as a duty to perform, an obligation to fulfill, or a chore to cross off their daily to-do list. Others discipline themselves to pray regularly, but they find the process tedious and tiresome.

I would like to help you see prayer in a new light. Think about it: We have access to the Creator of the universe. Through prayer we can tap into his power, might, and supernatural creativity. What's more, we can come to know our God more intimately and deeply as we communicate with him and listen as he speaks to us.

I like the way theologian Herbert Lockyer described prayer: "Is it not the desire, opportunity, and privilege of talking with God?" Desire. Opportunity. Privilege. Those three words form the foundation of a healthy perspective of prayer.

The Bible makes crystal clear the importance and significance of prayer. There are more than 650 prayers recorded in God's

Word—and more than 450 answers to prayer—not counting the entire book of Psalms, which is essentially a prayer book. Indeed, there are examples of prayers for virtually every situation you might face. As you look closely at biblical accounts, you will realize that people prayed in many different ways, and God's answers to those petitions were often surprising and unexpected.

GOD MAY NOT ALWAYS ANSWER OUR PRAYERS ON OUR TIMELINE.

Imagine: Talking with Your Creator!

The same holds true today. God may not always answer our prayers on our timeline or in the manner we would prefer. But when we need help, when we seek guidance, when we lack strength, we can know without doubt that God hears our prayers and will answer them according to his divine will and in his perfect timing. Whatever our need may be, he never fails to respond lovingly to our cries and requests.

Sir Isaac Newton, the brilliant science pioneer, said that he could look through his telescope and see millions and millions of miles into space. Then he added, "But when I lay the telescope aside and I go into my room and shut the door and get down on my knees in earnest prayer, I see more of heaven and feel closer to the Lord than if I were assisted by all the telescopes on the earth."

Indeed, prayer brings you to the heart of God, right into the throne room of heaven. It is supernatural, yet it is a natural activity. Wherever you are, you can start speaking to your Creator and enter into dialogue with him. Conversation with God should be part of daily life and an outflow of a grateful heart.

Sometimes new believers think they have to fold their hands, get on their knees, and use words like *thee* and *thou* in order to get God's attention. Of course, that's not true. God promises to hear us regardless of whether our prayers are eloquent or simple, brief or lengthy, motivated by praise or motivated by panic. The Old Testament saints remind us that we need to know very little about prayer in order to pray. They didn't talk much about the methodology and technique of prayer—they just prayed. They simply communicated with their Father in heaven, whom they trusted and revered.

As we embark on our exploration of prayer, I would like to highlight two foundational truths we can glean from the early chapters of the book of Genesis.

Prayer Brings Spiritual Awakening

In the Garden of Eden, before Adam and Eve sinned, prayer as we think of it wasn't necessary. The first man and woman quite literally walked with God in the garden and talked with him directly. What an awesome experience it must have been to converse face-to-face with the Creator!

But when Adam and Eve were deceived by Satan and sinned against God, a separation occurred. Because evil had entered the world, a chasm opened between God and his creation. Prayer, therefore, became the bridge that restored that communication. With that background in mind, let's pick up the story:

> *Adam lay with his wife again, and she gave birth to a son and named him Seth, saying, "God has granted me another child in place of Abel, since Cain killed him." Seth also had a son, and he named him Enosh. At that time men began to call on the name of the LORD (Gen. 4:25–26).*

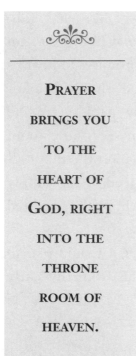

PRAYER BRINGS YOU TO THE HEART OF GOD, RIGHT INTO THE THRONE ROOM OF HEAVEN.

Some teachers suggest that this is where prayer began—that prayer was "invented" in the time of Enosh. But I believe this passage actually refers to *corporate* worship, when people joined together to speak with God. From the time that Adam and Eve's son Cain killed his brother Abel, darkness and evil began to pervade the human population. Cain left home and built a city, where he trained people to turn their backs on God. In fact, we can see that the first human government was created by people who had rebelled against God and wanted to run their lives without him. During that time period, there was no witness for the Lord—except when Adam and Eve had a third son, Seth, who in turn had Enosh. We don't know why, but somehow the birth of Enosh sparked a spiritual awakening. People began to call on the name of the Lord in prayer.

So in Genesis 4 we see a new generation discovering what it means to talk with God. And that is the first thing we should understand about prayer: *Prayer brings about spiritual awakening.* If you and I want to activate a spiritual transformation in our lives, if we want our eyes opened and our hearts stirred in new and fresh ways, that transformation will begin with prayer.

Prayer Leads to Spiritual Growth

Not long after Enosh, another fellow with a similar name appears on the scene. This man, Enoch, is also closely associated with prayer:

> *When Enoch had lived 65 years, he became the father of Methuselah. After he became the father of Methuselah, Enoch walked with God 300 years and had other sons and daughters. Altogether, Enoch lived 365 years. Enoch walked with God; then he was no more, because God took him away (Gen. 5:21–24).*

Enoch is quite an interesting character. We don't know much about him from these few verses in Genesis, but the New Testament gives us more information:

> *By faith Enoch was taken from this life, so that he did not experience death; he could not be found, because God had taken him away. For before he was taken, he was commended as one who pleased God (Heb. 11:5).*

Enoch shows up in another New Testament passage, this time in the book of Jude:

> *Enoch, the seventh from Adam, prophesied about these men: "See, the Lord is coming with thousands upon thousands of his holy ones to judge everyone, and to convict all the ungodly of all the ungodly acts they have done in the ungodly way, and of all the harsh words ungodly sinners have spoken against him" (Jude 14–15).*

Even though his complete biography comprises a total of eight verses, we learn some important truths about this man. We know that he was a preacher. More important, we are told that Enoch walked with God. In fact, he walked with the Lord for three hundred years. When his wife gave birth to Methuselah (who would become the oldest man on the planet), something happened to Enoch. At sixty-five years of age, he began a spurt of spiritual growth that lasted another three centuries.

The Hebrew word translated *walk* means "to go on habitually." So the Bible tells us that this man had communion—a close relationship—with God every day for three hundred years. He grew spiritually as he walked with the Lord and talked with him. If Enosh shows us that prayer brings spiritual awakening, Enoch shows us that *prayer brings spiritual growth—a continual, ongoing maturation in the faith.*

I can imagine Enoch getting up early in the morning, beginning his day with God, talking with him, telling him about the challenges he faced, and drawing strength from his relationship with the Lord. As we are open with God, in continual communication, sharing our problems and feelings with him, God will answer our prayers and lead us in the way that we should go. *If we keep praying, we will keep growing.*

Prayer Puts Life in Perspective

I have the privilege of serving as a police chaplain and reserve officer in San Diego. One night I was present when a shooting incident occurred. A man had taken a hostage at gunpoint and was holed up in an apartment. I tried to talk with the man for two hours, to reason with him and facilitate a peaceful resolution to the conflict. But there would be no heroics that night, no happy ending. Eventually, tensions escalated, and the man threatened police officers. It looked as if he would kill his hostage. So the SWAT team stormed in and fatally shot the gunman. A few hours later, I had the daunting task of talking with the man's widow.

The next day, I felt deeply anguished and grief-stricken. As I jogged along a deserted beach, I screamed out to God, "You've got to take this pain and ugliness!" After jogging and screaming for an hour, I was exhausted. I couldn't even walk home, so I called my daughter to come pick me up.

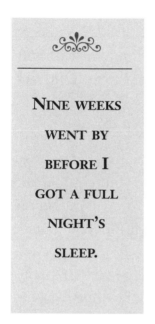

NINE WEEKS WENT BY BEFORE I GOT A FULL NIGHT'S SLEEP.

It was then that I received even more terrible news. My daughter told me that the son of dear friends of mine had just been killed in an auto accident along with two other young men. I had to call the parents, then drive several hours from San Diego to Palm Springs to meet with my friends and the parents of the other victims. That day I went from one shock to another. To say the least, I was deeply shaken and emotionally spent.

Nine weeks went by before I got a full night's sleep. But God used those weeks to prompt me to look within myself. In the night I would hear the voice of the gunman saying, *You could've done more. I wouldn't be dead now if you were a stronger Christian. I'm in hell, and you sent me here.*

The devil—the accuser—was tormenting me. But I kept on praying, and in time I began to see things differently. I thought about all the parents with children lying in the hospital. I thought of all the people who were suffering physical abuse, financial ruin, and broken relationships. I realized that there were many people going through much more pain than I was.

Through prayer and an ongoing relationship with God, he helps us put things into proper perspective. Our heavenly Father promises that he will not allow anything into our lives that will destroy us (see 1 Cor. 10:15). Pain and hardship are intended to make us stronger, to humble us, to make us more tenderhearted and gentle toward others. That's what happened to me during that agonizing period of my life. Though it was a time of great struggle, my faith grew stronger, and my relationship with God grew deeper.

That is the example of Enoch and the lesson available to each of us: As we walk with God, as we deepen our intimacy with him through prayer, we habitually grow. We are transformed into the likeness of his Son, Jesus Christ (see 2 Cor. 3:18).

Stay Close to God Through Prayer

My prayer is that God will use this book to start a fire in your heart and that the fire will spread through your family, your church, and your town. I pray that, as in the days of Enosh, you will call on the Lord, saying: "Father, I just want to tell you that I love you and I need you."

I also pray that you will walk with God and grow, habitually, day after day and year after year. I pray that if we meet twenty years from now, I will still be walking with the Lord, and so will you. I trust that we will be able to swap stories of miraculous answers to prayer and tell one another of our ever-deepening relationships with God. Sure, we will have endured disappointments and defeats, frustrations and failures—but we will still be walking steadfastly with the Lord, and that makes all the difference.

I agree wholeheartedly with Brennan Manning, who wrote:

> *Whatever else it may be, prayer is first and foremost*
> *an act of love. Before any pragmatic, utilitarian, or altruis-*
> *tic motivations, prayer is born of a desire to be with Jesus.*
> *His incomparable wisdom, compelling beauty, irresistible*
> *goodness, and unrestricted love lure us into the quiet of our*

*hearts where he dwells. To really love someone implies a
natural longing for presence and intimate communion.
(Manning 2003)*

Prayer causes us to stay close to the Lord and grow spiritually.
It is hard to get away from God—unless you stop talking with him.
If you stop communicating with your spouse, children, or friends,
your relationships are bound to suffer. You will drift apart and
become strangers. But continue talking and sharing, and your
relationships will grow stronger. The same is true with your relationship with God. Habitual, continual prayer—walking and talking with God—will cause you to grow closer to him.

CHAPTER TWO

CONVERSING WITH THE KING

"We should speak to God from our hearts
and talk to Him as a child talks to his father."
C. H. SPURGEON

In the movie "Bruce Almighty," comic actor Jim Carrey plays an angry, down-on-his-luck television newsman. After tiring of the newsman's complaints, God offers him the chance to take over the Almighty's job.

Something else unusual happens in this movie. God's phone number appears on the Carrey character's pager when the deity tries to call him. Although movies and TV shows typically use a phony 555 prefix, this time the seven-digit number displayed is real, at least for certain area codes.

As a result, all over the country, people started dialing their area code and then the number, leading some to fascinating interactions between callers and those who unwittingly acted as God's answering service.

One woman told the answering machine at the Radio Colorado Network, "I'm in jail right now. Like I said to you last night, 'I love you.'" She promised to go straight and prayed to be able to return to her husband and children.

Another caller said, "Hey, God, I've done some really bad things in my life, and I need to repent. So please answer my prayers."

Yet another caller said, "I know this isn't the number for God, but I'm calling to see if you have the other number."

In San Diego, where I live, callers who used the movie number got a business cell phone for Cathy Romano, president of a company that manages the practices of seventy physicians. After overcoming her initial irritation at getting forty or more calls a day from "Bruce Almighty" viewers, the busy executive started playing along.

"Hello, this is God," she answered one call, on a whim.

Her caller, a female, exclaimed, "I can't believe it! It's God—and it's a woman!" (Graham 2003)

What if we could really connect with God in this way? Would you like to be able to dial a number and talk with him? Well, I have news for you: He has given us ready access at any moment, from any location, in any circumstance in which we might find ourselves. And, of course, all we have to do is begin speaking to him, either silently or aloud. Our Father wants to communicate with his children so much that he has made it incredibly easy for them to make the connection.

God Is Waiting for Your Call

The book of Psalms contains 150 prayers—some long, some short, some joyful, some sorrowful. Many of the psalms were written by David, Israel's greatest king, who is described in the Bible as a man after God's own heart (see Acts 13:22).

In Psalm 145, David wrote, "The LORD is near to all who call on him, to all who call on him in truth. He fulfills the desires of those who fear him; he hears their cry and saves them" (vv. 18–19). The

THE KING IS

PRESENT

WITH US—

READY AND

WILLING TO

CONVERSE

WITH US.

Lord is indeed near, waiting for us to initiate contact with him. And when we do begin conversing with him, he hears—that is, he listens carefully and attentively. This theme was echoed by Isaiah, who spoke for the Lord, saying, "Before they call I will answer; while they are still speaking, I will hear" (Isa. 65:24). God knows what we need even before we come to him (see Matt. 6:8).

From these Scriptures and many others, we know that the King is present with us— ready and willing to converse with us. But it is amazing how many distractions there are to take our focus off of him. When we turn on the evening news, our attention becomes fixated on the latest crisis. When we watch our favorite sports team, we become absorbed in the competition in which it is engaged. When our children start throwing food at the dinner table or squabbling about something, naturally we feel that we must intervene. It's certainly not that God is going to vanish when our attention gets diverted; it's just that our thoughts and feelings shift elsewhere.

Still, we have this assurance: He is near, and he is eagerly waiting for us to re-engage with him in prayer. Our challenge is to continually come back to God with hearts and minds focused on him.

Opening Up to God

In his book *Strengthening Your Grip*, Charles Swindoll tells of a seventeenth-century Roman Catholic Frenchman named Francois Fenelon, who wrote these words:

Tell God all that is in your heart. As one unloads one's heart, its pleasures and its pains to a dear friend, tell Him your troubles that He may comfort you, tell Him your joys that He may sober them, tell Him your longings that He may purify them, tell Him your dislikes that He may help you conquer them, talk to Him of your temptations that He may shield you from them, show Him the wounds of your heart that He may heal them, lay bare your indifference to good, your depraved taste for evil, and your instability. Tell God how self-love makes you unjust to other people, how vanity tempts you to be insincere, how pride disguises you to yourself and to others also.

If you thus pour out all your weaknesses, your needs, and your troubles, there will be no lack of what to say. You'll never exhaust the subject. It is continually being renewed. People who have no secrets from each other never want for subjects of conversation. They do not weigh their words, for there is nothing to be held back. Neither do they seek for something to say; they talk out of the abundance of the heart without consideration, they say just what they think. Blessed are they who attain such a familiar, unreserved relationship with God. (Swindoll 1998)

START THE DIALOGUE BY OPENING UP AND TELLING GOD WHATEVER IS ON YOUR HEART.

That's the essence of prayer. Pretty simple, isn't it? Just begin an honest, candid conversation with God. Start the dialogue by opening up and telling God whatever is on your heart. Tell him about your troubles, your joys, your likes and dislikes. Let God speak back to you, so he can begin to temper your spirit and shape your character.

Another great writer, C. S. Lewis, put it succinctly: "We must lay before Him what is in us, not what ought to be in us." As we approach God with humility and genuineness, there is no need for pretense. There is no need for secrets. Simply lay out your thoughts and feelings before the throne of God and talk to him with a pure heart and an open mind.

David Opened Up His Heart to God

King David was not shy about sharing his emotions with God. He freely expressed joy and sadness, disappointment and delight. He is an excellent role model for our own prayer lives.

One of the best examples of this kind of open-heart prayer is Psalm 32, so let's examine several verses from that beautiful composition. The psalm begins, "Blessed is he whose transgression is forgiven, whose sin is covered" (v. 1 NKJV). David, who committed some big sins, knew that being open with God meant admitting faults and failures.

So why did he include both *transgression* and *sin* in the same sentence? Was he using repetition to emphasize a point? I think there is a slight difference between a transgression and a sin. Let's say there's a field that you know has some birds in it, and you want to go bird hunting. But there's a barbed wire fence around the field and a sign posted that says, "No Trespassing." You look around and don't see the landowner or any security guards, so you climb over the fence, even though you know you are not supposed to. That's a transgression. You know what you are supposed to do, but you don't do it. Instead, you do just the opposite.

Sin can happen all of a sudden. It is not always premeditated like a transgression; it is often spontaneous and impulsive. It is not your strong will saying, "I don't care if I'm not supposed to do this, I'm going to do it anyway." Sin is like what Billy Graham says about lust: When a man sees a beautiful woman walk by and he turns to look, that's not the sin; it's the *second* look that becomes a sin. Sin is falling short of God's standard of holiness and right-eousness in some area of life.

It is wonderful, though, to realize what David was saying to each of us: "You are a blessed person when your transgression is forgiven." All of us are like sheep that have gone astray. We have done that which is right in our own eyes, rather than that which is pleasing to God. That transgression or sin could cause a strain or separation in our relationship with God. Yet the psalmist said that we are blessed because our transgression is forgiven, and our sin is covered. Because of God's forgiveness, we are free to communicate with him just as though we had done nothing wrong.

THE LONGER WE STAY AWAY FROM HIM, THE WORSE WE FEEL.

David went on to say, "Blessed is the man whose sin the LORD does not count against him and in whose spirit is no deceit" (Ps. 32:2). Isn't that close to what Francois Fenelon said? As you pour out your heart through prayer to God and open a conver-sation with him, the deceit will begin to vanish. You will have no lies, because you a will not be hiding anything.

The Cost of Silence

Sometimes we feel guilty and remorseful about our behavior, so we avoid talking to God. But the longer we stay away from him, the worse we feel. Apparently, this happened to David, as we see in the words he poured out to the Lord:

When I kept silent, my bones wasted away through my groaning all the day long. For day and night, your hand was heavy upon me; my strength was sapped as in the heat of summer. Then I acknowledged my sin to you and did not cover up my iniquity. I said, "I will confess my transgressions to the LORD"—and you forgave the guilt of my sin (Ps. 32:3–5).

Maybe you have shut down the communication channels between you and God. You have kept silent, and there is something that just feels like it's hard inside of you. You feel that you can't get beyond where you are, even though you want to do so. Perhaps you are angry with God for something. You don't think it's right how you are being treated, and this may be an issue that goes back weeks or months or years. It's not that you are shaking your fist at God or cursing him, but you don't pray as much because your relationship with him is strained. Inside you feel as though your bones are growing old and the joy of living is gone.

If you have been remote and distant from God, the Lord would like you to break the silence. He wants you to establish communication with him once again. He wants your bones to stop growing old. He wants you to start living. When you go before the Lord in prayer, you bask in his radiant glory and beauty and you experience the abundant life he has promised to all those who come to him in faith (see John 10:10; Heb. 11:6). You enter his throne room, and there you find mercy and grace, peace and joy (see Heb. 4:16).

God usually will not scream and shout to get your attention. If he is calling you to re-establish communication with him, chances are he won't yell in your ear. He is more subtle and gentle than that. You may simply feel an urging, a longing, deep within you. You may feel the weight of his hand upon your shoulder.

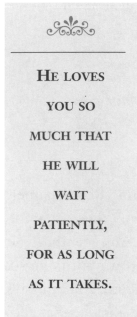

HE LOVES YOU SO MUCH THAT HE WILL WAIT PATIENTLY, FOR AS LONG AS IT TAKES.

Most parents understand that an authoritative *nonverbal* gesture is often more persuasive than shouting when a child needs correction. Sometimes a subtle act is more compelling than a forceful one. The child may not need to be spanked, sent to bed without dinner, or given a time-out. Often all the mom or dad has to do is walk up to the child and put a hand on his or her shoulder. That strong, imposing gesture commands attention, and change is usually forthcoming.

You may be feeling the heavy hand of God upon you. If so, he is calling you back to himself, and he is not going to let you go.

He loves you so much that he will wait patiently, for as long as it takes, to end the silence between you and him so that the two of you can begin communicating again.

God Is Near

As David continued to pour out his heart to the Lord, he said:

> *Let everyone who is godly pray to you while you may be found; surely when the mighty waters rise, they will not reach him. You are my hiding place; you will protect me from trouble and surround me with songs of deliverance (Ps. 32:6–7).*

God created you for his good pleasure and for fellowship with him (see Rev. 4:11 KJV). He has a purpose for your life and a path for you to follow, but underlying everything else is a love relationship with your Father. First and foremost, he wants to fellowship with you (1 John 1:3 KJV), and your fellowship with him will naturally activate and empower your gifts and talents.

So many people think, *I've got to do this or that to please God. I've got to accomplish something remarkable or he will be disappointed with me.* No, God just wants to fellowship with you, and being in his presence is enough.

When you are with God, enjoying his presence, you will be inspired to let the Holy Spirit flow out of you. As 1 John 1:6–7 (NKJV) says, "If we say that we have fellowship with Him, and walk in darkness, we lie and do not practice the truth. But if we walk in the light as He is in the light, we have fellowship with one another, and the blood of Jesus Christ His Son cleanses us from all sin." It is prayer that keeps us in fellowship with God and keeps us walking in the light.

Isn't that a long ways away from the condition David described in the first verses of Psalm 32? His vitality, strength, and joy were gone, and his bones were wasting away. He was trudging through life because he kept silent and wasn't talking to God. A godly person will pray when God is near, and the reward will be deep joy and increased vitality.

Delight in the Dialogue

In the midst of our hectic and harried lives, why should we pray? If there are hoards of people to help, goals to pursue, chores to get done, children to feed, why should we set aside time for prayer?

There are, of course, many reasons to spend regular, consistent time in prayer: so that we and our families will receive blessings, so that our ministries will be fruitful, so that we may have opportunities to serve God. Those reasons are all valid and proper.

But here is by far the most important reason we should pray: *so we can know God more intimately.* We deepen our relationship with our Father; we gain a better understanding of him, when we share our thoughts, feelings, and concerns with him.

I appreciate what writer John Guest said,

> *Just as husband and wife live out their lives against the backdrop of being married, so do we live out the entirety of our lives against the backdrop of a constant relationship with God. He is always there, always loving us, always ready to listen to us.*
>
> *As we recognize His unwavering commitment to us, we are able to live in the day-to-day adventure and challenge of His presence. We enjoy the dialogue. It's as if we say, "Oh, I must talk to Him about this!" (Guest and Sproul 1992)*

Yes, the very essence of the Christian life is a one-on-one relationship between our Creator and us. And prayer is the means by which we deepen that relationship and solidify that bond with him.

CHAPTER THREE

TO PRAY OR NOT TO PRAY?

"Every time we pray, our horizon is altered, our attitude to
things is altered—not sometimes but every time—and the
amazing thing is that we don't pray more."
OSWALD CHAMBERS

For many of us, making a concerted effort to communicate with God on a regular, consistent basis comes down to a Hamlet-like internal debate: *To pray or not to pray? That is the question.*

We look at our jam-packed day planners, we feel exhaustion deep in our bones, we experience stress born of too much to do in too few hours, and we struggle to devote time to prayer.

So let me get personal for a moment. Do you see prayer as an essential ingredient for a successful, meaningful life? Do you maintain an ongoing dialogue with God that is authentic, open, and enriching? Or do you squeeze in a quick prayer every now and then, maybe uttering a few words of thanks before a meal? Does it take a desperate situation to get you to pray?

Some time ago, I clipped a newspaper article about an Australian man named John Sokolenko, who was going through a divorce and who became despondent about separating from his wife. He tried to kill himself by ingesting poison, but he failed.

Then he took 156 painkiller tablets, and he survived that too.

Finally, he opened the valve on a propane tank and waited to be overcome by the fumes. After a while, he decided that wasn't going to work either. Forgetting about the fumes in the house, he lit a cigarette. The flame ignited the gas, causing a massive explosion that leveled the house. The man was thrown into the backyard by the blast. Aside from being dazed and a bit singed, he was unharmed. After all that, he figured that marriage is a risky business too, and that he might as well make the effort to patch things up with his wife. And, in fact, that's exactly what he did.

Isn't this what many of us do in regard to prayer? Problems keep getting worse and worse, so we figure it's time to turn to God. We say, "Okay, Lord, I get the message. I can't get out of this mess on my own, and I need your help." But the apostle Paul tells us to "pray without ceasing" (1 Thess. 5:17 NKJV). God wants us to talk with him all the time, not just when our circumstances go sour.

You have probably heard and perhaps even memorized the well-known passage from Matthew 7: "Ask and it will be given to you; seek and you will find; knock and the door will be opened to you. For everyone who asks receives; he who seeks finds; and to him who knocks the door will be opened" (vv. 7–8). This is a great promise to you and me. We have complete access to heaven, and that access will bring us in contact with the Creator of the universe.

Jesus' explanation of prayer is pretty simple really. First, he says to ask. There's no need to hesitate or hem and haw. Just state your request clearly and directly.

Second, he says that if you seek, you are going to find what you are looking for. God doesn't play games. If you are, with pure motives, seeking guidance or assistance, he will give it to you.

Third, Jesus says that if you simply knock, the door will be opened to you. You don't have to pound on the door. You don't

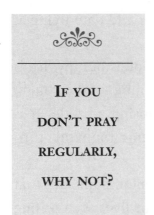

IF YOU

DON'T PRAY

REGULARLY,

WHY NOT?

have to shout and make a ruckus to awaken God. He is waiting for you, and as soon as he hears the slightest tap on the door, he will welcome you in for a heart-to-heart chat.

For Non-praying People: Open a Channel

If you don't pray regularly, why not? Maybe you have been telling yourself, "I'm not good enough to pray. I don't know how to pray. I don't know what I should pray for. God wouldn't want to hear my prayers anyway." Regardless of your reasons for not praying, now is an excellent time to begin using this precious gift God has given you.

Even a casual reading of the Bible will reveal that prayer is important to God. I did a little research and found that the word *pray* occurs 146 times in 139 verses in the Bible. The word *prayer* occurs 108 times, and many derivations appear as well. The word *prayers* occurs 27 times; *praying*, 25 times; *prays*, 5 times; and *prayed*, 59 times. So, according to *Strong's Exhaustive Concordance* (New King James Version) (Strong 1997) some form of the word *pray* is found in the Bible 370 times. That does not include other words or phrases with like meaning, such as *confess, plead,* or *call on the name of the Lord.* If a word shows up that often in the Bible, we should pay attention. God is obviously emphasizing a point. And in this case, the point is clear: Prayer is very significant to God, for that is how we develop a closer relationship with our heavenly Father.

One of the greatest joys I have is being a pilot. Sometimes when I am flying along on a beautiful day, I don't think about praying. There seems to be no reason to pray. The plane's engines are humming, the fuel gauges are up, the oil pressure is fine, the temperature level is good, the radio is zeroed in, and I am flying at the right altitude.

But then there are those times when the ride is bumpy, ice is building up on the wings, the engines are running a little rough, turbulence is jostling the aircraft, and I am losing altitude. It is amazing how quickly my thoughts turn toward prayer!

> THE LORD DOESN'T WANT US TO THINK THAT HE IS JUST THE BIG 911 IN THE SKY.

Even if you aren't a pilot, I am sure that you can relate. When our lives are cruising along smoothly, we don't feel the urgency to pray. But when storm clouds form and the ride gets bumpy, we suddenly remember to call on God for help.

Still, the Lord doesn't want us to think that he is just the big 911 in the sky, for emergency use only. He certainly will provide help when asked, according to the promises in his Word, but he wants far more than that from our relationship with him. He wants prayer to be the means by which we communicate and share our *entire* lives with him.

Jesus Talks to Non-praying People

Just as there are those today who don't pray, so there were people in Jesus' time who didn't pray. That's why he told a crowd of listeners:

> *"I tell you the truth, my Father will give you whatever you ask in my name. Until now you have not asked for anything in my name. Ask and you will receive, and your joy will be complete" (John 16:23–24).*

Jesus was aware that some people were asking nothing in his name. To the listeners of his day, and to us centuries later, he has said to approach God with the assurance of being heard and answered. He has given us a key—his name—that allows us to open the door to heaven and begin to converse with God.

You may say, "But I can't talk to God. Why would he want to listen to me?" The truth is that God is already listening to you.

During the 1960s, before I was a Christian, I hitchhiked across the United States. For a couple of months, I lived in a dumpy hotel in a small town outside of Chicago. My room, which cost ten dollars a week, was above a tavern. I found a job in a machine shop, and I would get up at 5:00 A.M. when the windchill factor was twenty degrees below zero.

At night, I would sit in a tavern to pass the lonely hours. I had no friends and didn't know anyone there. Beer was a dime, whiskey was thirty-five cents a shot, and a cheeseburger was forty-five cents. I would stack up the beer mugs and the whiskey shot glasses from 6:00 until 11:00 P.M. until I was ready to pass out. Then I would head upstairs, go to sleep, get up at 5:00 A.M., and follow the same routine again—night after night and day after day for a couple of months.

One night a huge storm broke loose outside of Chicago, and I was at my typical spot, slumped over on a barstool, drunk. I remember walking out of the tavern thoroughly depressed, staggering through the neighborhood, feeling utterly alone, with no jacket or raincoat or umbrella. I stumbled around, soaking wet, crying out at the top of my lungs, "Where are you, God? If there really is a God, why am I so empty and lonely? I need your help! Are you up there? Can you hear me?"

Today, I realize that he *was* listening. He knew I was in desperate need and in deep trouble. He was waiting for me. But I did not know that access to him was through his Son, Jesus Christ. Unfortunately, it took me a while to figure that out.

Eventually, I returned to Southern California, and I can remember sitting stoned out of my brains at Newport Beach in the middle of the night, looking up at the stars and crying out to God. Other times, I would go out to the desert and wait for flying saucers to come down, pick me up, and take me out of my misery. I would scream to God, "If you're out there, where are you? How will I ever find you?"

He heard those desperate pleas, and he was arranging things so that I would bump into the person who would first tell me about Jesus Christ. He was arranging things so that I would bump into the person who would say, "Mike, come to church with me." He was also arranging things so that I would hear his Word preached and would understand his message of love for the first time.

Still you may be saying, "How can I talk to God? I'm not a good person. I've got so many problems—things I don't want to admit. God doesn't want to talk to a person like me. Maybe he'll listen if I clean up my act."

That is not what Jesus meant when he said, "My Father will give you whatever you ask in my name. Until now you have not asked for anything in my name." He was simply saying to ask. He was also telling us, "I'm aware that you've never asked anything." If you are a non-praying person, it is important to understand that God is inviting you to pray, and he is listening.

As if that is not amazing enough, Jesus has sweetened the deal. He has said that

AT NIGHT, I WOULD SIT IN A TAVERN TO PASS THE LONELY HOURS.

when you ask anything in his name, "You will receive, and your joy will be complete." That is the blessing of answered prayer—it brings a *fullness* of joy into your life that you can't get anywhere else.

For Praying People: Keep Going and Keep Growing

The apostle Paul guided and nurtured several fledgling churches, and he taught the people under his tutelage to pray. What's more, he encouraged those who prayed to *keep on praying*. In a letter to the church in Rome, he wrote:

> *Love must be sincere. Hate what is evil; cling to what is good. Be devoted to one another in brotherly love. Honor one another above yourselves. Never be lacking in zeal, but keep your spiritual fervor, serving the Lord. Be joyful in hope, patient in affliction,* faithful in prayer *(Rom. 12:9–12, emphasis added).*

In another letter, this one to the Christians in the city of Colosse, Paul wrote, "Devote yourselves to prayer, being watchful and thankful" (Col. 4:2). Paul apparently knew the human tendency to get careless and casual about prayer, so he emphasized again and again the need for diligence.

Prayer is a key to spiritual growth. It is hard to imagine any Christian growing very much for very long without a consistent prayer life. That's why Paul emphasized the importance of prayer even to those who were already praying, saying, in essence, "Keep on praying, so you can keep on growing."

That same message is as applicable now as it was then. If your prayer life is steadfast and unwavering, that's outstanding. Now keep going and keep growing.

Watch Your Motives

Have you been praying but not receiving the answers you are looking for? The New Testament writer James tells us why this may be:

> *When you ask, you do not receive, because you ask with wrong motives, that you may spend what you get on your pleasures (James 4:3).*

This is reminiscent of the way the Old Testament prophet Jeremiah sized up the human condition: "The heart is deceitful above all things, and desperately wicked; who can know it?" (Jer. 17:9 NKJV). The purpose and intent underlying our prayers—*the reasons* we are praying—are vitally important.

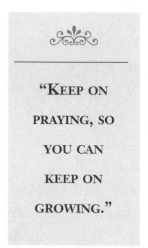

"KEEP ON PRAYING, SO YOU CAN KEEP ON GROWING."

It is clear from God's Word that he delights in giving his children blessings, but it is also clear that he is not a genie who will grant our every wish. We may pray, "God, please give me that promotion at work," not so we can have a more strategic position in which to witness for Christ, but because we want more power and prestige. We may pray, "Lord, help this deal to go through," not because we think it will glorify God, but because it will bring us lots of money to spend on our own pleasures.

It may be that you are asking and not receiving because your prayers are missing the mark, which is what the Greek word for *sin* means. (Vine 1996) When our motives are off target, our prayers will be too. They will not be "aimed" properly. God is not going to encourage us in this selfish kind of praying, so we are not going to get what we ask for. God does not want to spoil us; he wants to build character in us.

The *Los Angeles Times* featured an interview with a Southern California psychiatrist who said that four out of five teenagers or young adults visiting his medical center had a psychological sickness he could not cure. Why?

"Each of them demands that his world conform to *his* uncontrolled desires," he explained. "Society has provided them with so many escape routes that they never have to stand their ground against disappointment or against postponement of pleasure, and the weight of responsibility."

All three of these forces—disappointment, postponement of pleasure, and weight of responsibility—shape character. The psychiatrist added, "If the personality disorder persists far into adulthood, there will be a society of pleasure-driven people hopelessly insecure and dependent."

And that is where America is today—insecure and dependent on Big Brother. God's intent for our lives is continually to shape and mold us into the image of his Son, Jesus (see Rom. 8:28–29). In short, he wants our character, our heart attitude, to become more and more like his. And he uses prayer as a means to accomplish that transformation in our lives.

The Most Important Decision

So much of life comes down to the choices we make. We can choose to get up and go to work rather than call in sick. We can choose to study for an exam rather than loaf in front of the TV. We can choose to spend time with our children rather than put in more hours at the office. And we can choose whether or not to spend time in prayer. That may very well be the most critical decision we make on a daily basis.

YOU CANNOT HANDLE MANY OF THE THINGS THIS WORLD THROWS AT YOU, BUT YOUR GOD CAN.

You cannot handle many of the things this world throws at you, but your God can. Your God does hear prayer, your God does answer prayer, and your God is mighty and powerful. His Son is the Lord of all lords and the King of all kings (see Rev. 17:14). The Bible says that at the name of Jesus Christ every knee in heaven and earth shall bow, and every tongue shall confess that Jesus Christ is Lord to the glory of God (see Phil. 2:10–11).

If you are not a praying person now, let me remind you that it is that same Jesus who says to you, "Until now you have not asked for anything in my name. Ask and you will receive, and your joy will be complete." If you are a praying person, God's Word says to you, be "steadfast in prayer" (see Col. 4:2 ASV).

If you want to grow spiritually, you must pray consistently. It is as simple as that. Give it the attention it deserves, and you will fall in love with prayer.

CHAPTER FOUR

THE PRIORITY OF PRAYER

*"If you have so much business to attend to
that you have no time to pray,
then you have more business on your hands
than God ever intended you to have."*

D. L. MOODY

Prayer is not a casual, take-it-or-leave-it activity. God intends that prayer be at the core of our relationship with him. Through prayer, we express the deepest longings of our hearts and seek God's help for our most pressing needs.

When you are a busy homemaker with children to tend to, rooms to clean, meals to prepare, and schedules to keep, life can become quite hectic. I know—I watched my wife Sandy juggle all of the above and do a great job of it.

With five small children under ten years of age and a husband who was ministering to a large congregation and guiding a ministry team, Sandy's life had more demands than a porcupine has quills. Her prayer life was a necessary part of her every waking moment.

I remember reading the prayer strategy of John Wesley's mother, who was extremely busy with many children and a minister-husband.

When she was exhausted from the toils of household labor and family needs, she would simply pull her apron over her head in their small house and sit down to pray. The children were taught never to disturb her in that most interesting position. That was Mother's quiet time and prayer time with God.

It doesn't matter if you are a busy pastor of a "megachurch" or a mother of ten with all the duties that come with the job description. People with lots of responsibilities and long to-do lists—which includes most folks these days—usually learn quickly that time is the most important commodity of their lives. Therefore, they must become skilled at protecting their time and using it wisely; otherwise, it will easily get frittered away.

In a private meeting with Billy Graham several years ago, I asked the great evangelist and spiritual leader about his personal prayer life. One of the things he said caught my attention in a powerful way, because it was the same answer my pastor Chuck Smith gave me years ago: *Pray unceasingly.* We may set aside special times for intense prayer, but we should also keep up a running dialogue with God throughout each day.

I have counseled hundreds of people over the years, and many times I have asked about their prayer lives. Inevitably, those individuals who were in the most trouble and were most desperate for help were those who said those famous last words, "I just don't have time to pray."

> IN ALL REALITY, WE DON'T HAVE TIME *NOT* TO PRAY.

In all reality, we don't have time *not* to pray. In my life, I have found that time for prayer is a top priority, an absolute must. Without it, I am lost and do not have a sharp edge in my ministry, family relationships, or friendships. Prayer keeps me focused on who *I* am in respect to who *God* is. Prayer keeps me keenly aware that I am a servant of the King, and that he has given me everything I have. Any recognition I may receive for community service or effective ministry is due entirely to the fact that I am his servant.

Leading by Example

Again and again in the accounts of the life of Jesus, we see that prayer, communication with his Father, was at the center of all he did. For instance, we read in the first chapter of Mark that Jesus had a busy day interacting with multitudes of people who were crowding around him to hear his words and see his miracles. Then he taught at the synagogue in Capernaum, where he cast out an unclean spirit. Afterward, he went to the house of Simon and Andrew, where he found that Simon's mother-in-law was sick with a fever. So he healed her.

Clearly, Jesus was doing many important things, and the frantic pace of his ministry didn't stop when night fell:

> *That evening after sunset the people brought to Jesus all the sick and demon-possessed. The whole town gathered at the door, and Jesus healed many who had various diseases. He also drove out many demons. ...*
>
> *Very early in the morning, while it was still dark, Jesus got up, left the house and went off to a solitary place, where he prayed. Simon and his companions went to look for him, and when they found him, they exclaimed: "Everyone is looking for you!" (Mark 1: 32–37).*

Jesus had spent all day and all evening ministering to people, touching their hearts, healing their pains, soothing their hurts. We are not sure if he left the house immediately after the last person from the town had been healed, or if he caught a few hours of sleep first. But we do know that before daybreak—before the sun had even begun to peek over the horizon—he was out in a lonely, solitary place to pray.

I can imagine his disciples waking up and looking around for him. They probably said to each other, "Have you seen Jesus? Where do you think he went? We had better go look for him." So they started wandering the surrounding countryside and eventually found him alone, praying.

Jesus decided on that day, when he was surely exhausted from all the work that he had done before, to get up before daybreak. He probably knew that the people in the fishing village would start getting up before sunrise. He was no doubt aware that the local fishermen would be getting their boats ready to go out on the Sea of Galilee. He likely knew that their wives would be preparing breakfast and getting the younger children ready for school and the older ones ready to work in the house or fields. Jesus no doubt knew that he had to be ahead of the crowds. So he arose earlier than anyone else and went out and found a lonely wilderness spot where he could be alone with his heavenly Father.

Apparently, it wasn't long before the disciples found him. "Everyone is looking for you," they said. It is almost as if they were saying, "What are you doing out here in the middle of nowhere? There are people to teach, sick folks to heal, the demon-possessed to set free. You've got appointments to keep." Jesus knew his source of strength, encouragement, and guidance, which is why he "went off to a solitary place, where he prayed."

Jesus demonstrates to all of us that prayer is so important we need to make time for it intentionally. All of us are busy, and our calendars are full. We must find time for prayer—even if it means cutting out other important things. But we need to do more than

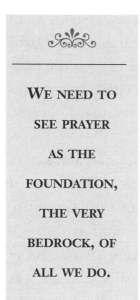

WE NEED TO SEE PRAYER AS THE FOUNDATION, THE VERY BEDROCK, OF ALL WE DO.

simply *schedule* time *for* prayer—we need a fundamental shift in our *attitude toward* prayer. We need to see prayer as the foundation, the very bedrock, of all we do.

Prayer Keeps Us in the Light

For some reason, miracles seem to happen more often in countries other than the United States. In Asia and elsewhere in the world, there are frequent reports of sick people being physically healed and troubled people being delivered from demons. I think the reason this happens more frequently outside the United States is because the people in many foreign countries are unencumbered with the need to figure out everything mentally and logically; they just sense that God is there with them and among them. They don't need to have a rational explanation for everything that happens; they just let the Spirit of God work among them as he wills.

Some years ago, I was part of a large outreach in Guadalajara, Mexico. One night the outdoor arena in the city's park was full of people, thousands of them. It was standing room only. My pastor, Chuck Smith, had flown in to be with us, pray with us, and speak at the pastors' conference we were holding. He had never attended one of our international outreaches before, and I wanted him to be impressed with what we were doing. So I had prepared what I thought was the greatest three-point evangelistic sermon ever. I had gone over this sermon for hours, and I knew that Billy Graham himself would have been in awe of it.

All of us involved had "bathed" the event in prayer, asking God to work miracles in that place. But when it came time for me to preach, the devil literally blew up the public address system. All of the electrical cords connecting the microphones to the soundboard were fried. I could see sparks flying from where I sat on the platform. The lights went out in the arena, the main circuit box caught fire, and everything was fused together. There was no way I could preach. I couldn't believe it!

All I could do was throw out my brilliant sermon and say to the crowd as loudly as I could, "You have heard the Gospel of Jesus Christ through the music played in the last thirty minutes, from all of these artists who have been up here sharing through song. You have heard that Jesus Christ is the King, that he is the Son of God, that he died on a cross for your sins, that he was buried in a grave, and that he rose from the dead. He wants you to repent of your sins; if you do that, he will give you eternal life. So all of you who want to accept Jesus Christ and receive eternal life, come forward now. Make your way up here even in the dark."

Hundreds and hundreds came forward. I looked at my watch—my extemporaneous altar call had taken maybe five minutes. Then I sat down. *Well,* I thought, *so much for my fantastic sermon!*

When it was all over, I said to Chuck, "I had the greatest three-point evangelistic sermon you would have ever heard."

"Well," he said, "it looks like the Lord did better than that, Mike."

That, of course, is how it should have been. Chuck and everyone present that night were impressed with the moving of the Spirit of God in that place, and certainly not with my impromptu altar call. We had prayed diligently that the Lord would work through that outreach, and once again he had triumphed over the devil's schemes.

Tapping into the Power Source

My experience in Guadalajara reminded me of a famous quote by the late Charles Spurgeon, who is known throughout the world as the prince of preachers. He once said, "I would rather teach one man to pray than ten men to preach."

When Spurgeon was just a young man, in his early twenties, he preached without a PA system to 25,000 people at a time. The entire city of London loved him. There was standing room only at every service in which he spoke. He also held a pastor's college at his church, where he trained hundreds of men to be effective teachers and ministers. Yet this preacher of preachers knew that prayer is the essential ingredient of any kind of ministry.

With prayer undergirding our outreach to mankind, we have a power source flowing straight from heaven. That's why another respected Christian leader, Andrew Murray, once said, "The man who mobilizes the Christian church to pray will make the greatest contribution to world evangelization in history."

Developing a Proper Attitude Toward Prayer

One of the most exemplary men of prayer in the New Testament was the apostle Paul. In a letter to Timothy, his protégé in the faith, Paul wrote, "Therefore I desire that the men pray everywhere, lifting up holy hands, without wrath and doubting" (1 Tim. 2:8 NKJV). In this concise verse, Paul tells us three things that will empower our prayer lives.

First, pray everywhere. We can pray out on the ball field, on a surfboard or motorcycle, in karate class or the midst of a tennis match, during a city council meeting or while taking a test. Anywhere we may find ourselves, we can maintain an ongoing dialogue with the King.

Second, we are to pray while lifting up holy hands. It is not the position of the body that God is looking for; it is the position of the heart. Paul's instruction has nothing to do with our posture and everything to do with our purity. Lifting up holy hands implies total surrender: "My life is yours, God, and it is in that spirit of humility and gratitude that I come to you. I want to glorify you and tell you how much I love you."

We are to lift up holy hands without wrath. Too often when we talk to God, we are angry. We may be mad at somebody—our boss, our landlord, or our neighbor. We may be nursing a grudge toward someone who has wronged us. This is the kind of "heart condition" to which Paul is referring here. When we pray, we can lift up holy hands without any wrath inside of us and say, "Lord, why should I be angry at another human being who is one of your creatures just as I am? Please give me more compassion and grace." With his help, we can be more patient with people. We can be more accepting. We can realize that God calls us to love all people, just as he does.

PAUL TELLS US TO PRAY WITH CONFIDENCE AND CERTAINTY. THAT IS THE ATTITUDE GOD WANTS US TO HAVE.

Third, Paul tells us that we should pray without doubting. How often do we pray but doubt that the Lord is going to answer our request? How often do we think, *Well, I'll ask, but I'm not sure God can do what I ask. Can God get me an extra twenty dollars this week? I'm not too sure. Where would God get an extra twenty dollars? Can the Lord help me patch up the rift in my relationship? Oh, the Lord's too busy to get involved in my little squabbles. My problems and my life situation are way beyond anything God has ever seen.*

Paul tells us to pray with confidence and certainty. That is the attitude God wants us to have—to *know* that he is going to answer. We don't know *how* he is going to answer, or *when* he is going to answer, or *where* he is going to answer. But we know without a doubt that he *will* answer.

Prompted to Pray

When prayer is a priority in our lives, we often sense the Holy Spirit prompting us to pray. We may be at work and suddenly feel the urge to pray for a friend who is in trouble. We may be driving on the freeway and know that we should start praying. We may not always know why we feel compelled to pray. There may be an accident about to happen up the road or one that has already happened behind us.

A recent Thanksgiving weekend was full of tragedies in San Diego, where I live. Three deadly fires erupted in three consecutive days, and that was just after a week of out-of-control brush fires that destroyed more than a hundred homes. Driving in my car that week, I heard on the radio a news report of an elderly woman who had died in a house fire started by a smoldering garbage can. That news report was interrupted by the story of a small corporate jet that had crashed a hundred miles north of us in Orange City at the John Wayne Airport. My immediate thought was for the moms, dads, and children who had lost family members in that accident. God brought those thoughts to my mind, and I prayed.

My point is that there are problems and crises around us every day, and these situations need our prayers. When prayer is of prime importance to us, we will often feel the Holy Spirit leading us to intercede for others before the God who is able to heal the hurts and calm the fears of the world.

Prayer must be our top priority. It is a must for everyone—popes, priests, and pastors; moms, dads, and kids; bosses, workers, and supervisors; generals, prime ministers, and presidents. No one is above the law, and in the same sense no one is above the gift and responsibility of prayer.

Discipline yourself to set the priority of prayer on your calendar. Start today by taking out your day planner and writing PRAYER on every day of the coming month. Then as the days pass by, erase those that you did not "have the time" to pray. You can then set some specific goals by seeing what priority you have given to prayer.

It takes time to pray, and we must devote time to prayer. Jesus, rising before the break of dawn, went to a solitary place, and there he prayed. Let us follow his example.

THE BUILDING BLOCKS OF PRAYER AND FAITH

"Every great movement of God can be traced to a kneeling figure."
D L. MOODY

We all have building blocks in our lives. Not the toy blocks that we used to build things with as children, but situations, occupations, relationships, educational opportunities, and so many other things that, taken together, help us develop into mature individuals.

Jesus believed in the principle of building blocks. He taught concerning the choices we have when we build a house or build our lives: "Therefore everyone who hears these words of mine and puts them into practice is like a wise man who built his house on the rock. The rain came down, the streams rose, and the winds blew and beat against that house; yet it did not fall, because it had its foundation on the rock" (Matt. 7:24–25).

In this chapter I would like to describe some of the building blocks that God used in my life, with special emphasis on the role of prayer. I am a living witness of the fact that God launches ministry and empowers it through prayer. I hope that God will use the following pages to give you a new appreciation for God's building blocks in your life, and to encourage you to fall in love with prayer.

Music, Music, Music

I have always loved music. It has been part of my life since child-hood. Growing up, I thought the trumpet was the coolest-looking instrument and the center of attention in the big bands of the time. So, in my childhood and adolescence I took trumpet lessons for several years.

Harry James was the most popular trumpet player during my youth. I vividly remember that a friend of mine got Harry James to autograph a photograph of himself playing the trumpet. Then my friend gave it to me as a gift. I was only in the fourth grade, so you can imagine the tremendous impact this had on a ten-year-old kid. My oldest brother, David, loved jazz, so I also grew up listening to the likes of George Shearing or the great jazz singer and trumpet player Louis Armstrong.

On top of that, my mother has a zest and zeal for music. She has never taken a piano lesson, yet she can sit down at the piano and play boogie-woogie or rhapsodies with ease. In the 1950s, when television sets were small and a rabbit-ear antenna sat on top of each set, bringing in fuzzy reception that could be viewed only in black and white, there was a quiz show called *Name That Tune*. My mother could name every song that was played, whistled, or hummed. My mom was up-to-date on big band, jazz, ballads, symphonies, you name it—even the emerging Elvis Presley songs of the day were no strangers to her.

I was a freshman in high school, about fourteen years old, when I realized that the trumpet was not going to be part of my life anymore. We had just finished band practice, and I was out the door, down the hallway, to my science lab before the bell rang, and I would get another tardy. It was then and there, in the midst of all the cute girls, that I felt my first awkwardness as a teenage boy. I realized that walking with a big black trumpet case hanging from my arm was not the "cool" or "in" look. Later, as the guitar became the instrument of choice, I began picking and strumming a bit, but I never lost my love for music.

Maranatha! Music

God used this love for music to draw me into an area of ministry that needed help and attention. There was a fledging new ministry outreach of Calvary Chapel of Costa Mesa, California. I had been a Christian for only a year and a half when I became involved as an administrator of this wonderful ministry, known as Maranatha! Music.

Looking back on that time in my life, I can see that it took me a while to realize what God was doing by placing me in that position. What I thought was a stepping-stone actually had nothing to do with arranging concerts for musicians, going to Hollywood and meeting with ASCAP (American Society of Composers, Authors and Publishers), and setting up a publishing company. I thought at first it was all about going to record companies and learning how to press records or establish retail and wholesale outlets for the music that was being produced.

In retrospect, it was none of that. In fact, the ministry aspect was not God's primary concern at all. God was using this time in music as a building block in my life. I was his student, and he was using the arena of ministry to train me and teach me his ways.

Are you familiar with Psalm 32:8–9? In it God says: "I will instruct you and teach you in the way you should go; I will guide you with My eye. Do not be like the horse or like the mule, which have no understanding, which must be harnessed by bit and bridle, else they will not come near you" (NKJV).

This verse jumped out at me as if it were designed just for me. I was in God's ministerial training program. I had been a free spirit, wandering wherever I wanted to go; God would take that wandering spirit and train it to have faith and to be willing to go in any direction he chose. The Lord of all creation was going to teach me to pray. And he would teach me that through prayer I would be able to know and understand his will for my life and for the ministry he had designed for me to fulfill.

There are three major items on God's agenda in this Scripture: *instruct, teach,* and *give direction.* It is often difficult to understand the "how-tos" of any challenge we take on. In this passage God promises to give each of us his personal attention and counsel.

Here is what I have found interesting after following his lead for so many years: He will use his *eye* to *guide* us.

Let me give you an example to illustrate this type of guidance. Say you and I are in the middle of a group of people, with everyone talking. If I want to point out something to you, but I don't want to interrupt the conversation, I can catch your eye—even if you are across the room—and then flick my eyes in the direction I want you to look. You will get the message loud and clear—without my having to say a word.

In the same manner, God can lead and guide us with "eye contact." But that means we have to be looking at his face. This is obviously a very personal means of communication, and David uses this expression in Psalm 32 to remind us that God is personal and intimate, not impersonal and remote. His Son, Jesus Christ, is our *personal* Lord and Savior.

Only through prayer can we develop this intimate, personal relationship that allows us to have eye-to-eye contact with him. It is from this vantage point that he will instruct us, teach us, and give us the personal direction we need for our life.

Without a doubt, I learned stewardship during those days with Maranatha! Music. I learned how to balance a budget, pay bills on time, develop new management and business skills—all experiences that helped me grow up and mature as a young man. But the main lessons I learned were about prayer. That was the most important building block in my life in those early years of ministry.

The Brook Cherith

As an intern minister I earned $75 per week; after one year of overseeing Maranatha! Music, I was making $150 per week—and that was when I had three children and a wife to support. Through those lean times God taught me to trust him for the basics of life. If there was ever anything beyond that, I would always know that it was God's abundance in our lives. That's why I call this early time in my development as a minister my "Brook Cherith" days. The name comes from an experience in the life of the prophet Elijah:

> *Then the word of the LORD came to him, saying, "Get away from here and turn eastward, and hide by the Brook Cherith, which flows into the Jordan. And it will be that you shall drink from the brook, and I have commanded the ravens to feed you there." So he went and did according to the word of the LORD, for he went and stayed by the Brook Cherith, which flows into the Jordan. The ravens brought him bread and meat in the morning, and bread and meat in the evening; and he drank from the brook (1 Kings 17:2–6 NKJV).*

In such times, with limited personal funds, I learned to pinch pennies and stretch dollars in order to put food on our table each day. It was always a miracle for me to behold, and actually these many years later I still marvel. Also, it kept my focus on the Lord as the supplier of everything the Macintosh household would ever need. And when it came to ministry funds, it taught me how to manage God's business and watch closely for waste and frivolous spending.

By the time I was ready to become a pastor in San Diego, God had taught me many practical lessons that I understood without any question or doubt. He had given me a business course, a faith course, and a prayer course all in one. I thought I was the "director of Maranatha! Music." How wrong I was. That experience wasn't just God's way of letting me enjoy music, inspire writers and musicians to record the first ever praise album, and begin a new wave of Christian music. He was looking thirty years into the future.

THESE LESSONS HAVE STUCK WITH ME FOR MORE THAN THREE DECADES NOW. OUR MINISTRY ALWAYS LOOKS TO GOD TO RAISE THE MONEY FOR HIS WORK.

Many days I would be on my knees, alone in my office, praying one by one for each music group at Calvary Chapel, praying for each musician and singer and their family members. I learned to pray for the phone bill, the stationery printing bill, the postage stamps, gas for the van to haul musicians and equipment to concerts. I learned to pray for auditorium rentals, lighting and sound rentals, posters, flyers, and hamburgers and french fries. When you don't have money for a ministry or a business, you *need* to pray. That's the lesson I learned.

These lessons have stuck with me for more than three decades now. Our ministry always looks to God, not to man or clever monthly mailers, to raise the money for his work. If it is God's work, then he will pay for it. And if God's people are spiritual, they know whom and what to support without someone twisting their arms and making them feel guilty about their giving to the Lord's work.

When you don't have medical insurance—and we didn't—you learn to pray when your three children are sick. And when you have appendicitis and no means to go to the hospital, you learn to pray.

As I look back on those experiences, I can see that God allowed hardship in the physical realm to develop me in the spiritual realm. As human beings, it is our nature to complain and grumble when we don't have the things we want or think we need. When we don't understand everything going on around us, we can become bitter and disenchanted with our surroundings or our job. But with God on our side, we can become prayer warriors. We can learn to communicate with heaven and "get the lowdown"—when we "get down low" before the throne of God.

Ministry in San Diego

My wife Sandy and I lived in an old farmhouse in Santa Ana, California. Behind it was a two-story duplex, which we rented to friends. Chuck and Carol Butler rented the downstairs unit for $75 per month, and Don Abshere rented the upstairs unit for $75 per month. The total payment for our loan was $183 per month, so with the rental income we actually paid $33 per month for a fifty-year-old, four-bedroom, two-bath farmhouse with orange and avocado trees surrounding it!

You see, God uses everything in our lives to teach us that he is in charge and that he is taking care of us. Although Sandy and I received only a small salary, heaven compensated by providing us a low monthly payment to live in a house that was more than adequate for our needs.

Monday Night Bible Study

Don is a jovial, happy man and a dear friend. He was a young Christian, very zealous to learn and teach the Bible. Rising early every morning, around 4:00 A.M., Don would set out into the community to earn his living as an accomplished carpenter and framer. At night, as tired as he was, he would attend every church service and every class I taught.

He had been invited by friends to come to San Diego and teach a Bible study to five people who had just left the hippie world and drug scene. They met and prayed every Monday night, and they wanted their friend Don to come and teach them. So every Monday afternoon, Don would show up at our back door and ask Sandy and me to pray for him and lay hands on him for the two-hundred-mile round-trip, as well as for the study with this group of excited young Christians.

He would always say, "Mike, do you want to come with me and speak?"

"No, Don, a two-hundred-mile round-trip, for five people?" I would reply. "No way, I'm too busy teaching and traveling and overseeing the ministry."

Little did anyone know that those five-minute Monday afternoon prayer times by our back door would change tens of thousands of lives in the future. Mine was to be the most challenged and changed of all of them.

A Sixteen-week Commitment

For months, Don invited me down to San Diego. Each time the answer I gave him was the same. But after a few months, there were ten to fifteen people gathering for the study. It wasn't that I refused to go somewhere for ten or fifteen people; it was just that I had so many other responsibilities at the time that the San Diego meeting just wasn't something that would fit into my already overly committed schedule.

Yet for some reason, I finally made a commitment to drive to San Diego and teach the Monday night study. No one sent me to do it; in reality, I was unknowingly being led by the Holy Spirit to enter into a special realm that God had prepared for me before the foundation of the earth (see Eph. 1:4). Besides which, I reasoned, if I did teach for a few weeks, then I wouldn't have to hear Don keep inviting me week after week.

My commitment was a simple one for this small group. I would teach one chapter from the Gospel of Mark each week for sixteen weeks, starting the first Monday evening in June 1974 and finishing the last week of September. I would help the group get a basic understanding of the Bible and develop a love for the person of Jesus Christ. Then I would "be about my Father's business" (Luke 2:49 KJV) back in my own neighborhood, a hundred miles to the north.

They were a fun group of people, all of them in their twenties. They wanted to grow spiritually and to know God personally. Unknown as yet to them or me, God was about to take this small group and do something with them and through them as phenomenal as anything recorded in the book of Acts. We began every Bible study with prayer and ended with prayer. But from the beginning, I always let people know that they could pray together and, as the Bible teaches, pray for one another. Indeed, prayer was a cornerstone of that group from the start.

Prayer in the Living Room

It soon became apparent to me that as this small group prayed for each other and their individual situations, walls between them began coming down. Prayer in a small group like this one fosters

PRAYER IN A SMALL GROUP FOSTERS OPENNESS AND TRANSPARENCY.

openness and transparency. As individual members of the group hear others share their hearts with God, it draws them closer to one another. Not only was the living room where we were meeting filled with singing, Bible study, and the building of friendships, it was also filled with prayer.

As usual, God had a plan that was so beyond me that I would not have believed it if he had told me. In three months, we had grown to about seventy-five people. I grabbed the opportunity to teach them personal evangelism. I challenged them to pass out 150 flyers. The next Monday night we would meet in the auditorium of a junior high school.

They took up the challenge and passed out the flyers, and the next week we had 150 in the auditorium. That week I had 300 flyers printed up and gave them to that crowd, informing them that we would return and use the same auditorium. This was a thrilling time for me to pray and see whether the new believers would go and tell their friends about Jesus Christ and his love for them.

Prayer in the House of Hospitality

Sure enough, the following Monday night there were three hundred people sitting in that auditorium listening to the music, studying the Bible, and praying with perfect strangers. This turn of events made us leave our comfort zone and move out of the living-room atmosphere and rent an auditorium in what is known as the House of Hospitality, in the center of Balboa Park in downtown San Diego. (Balboa Park is where the world-famous San Diego Zoo is located.)

We began with a few dozen people praying as a team before and after the Bible study. The results were, and continue to be, unbelievable. In the six-month period from the first study, we had grown to five hundred people in the old auditorium in the park.

Some nights there would be people sitting on the floor and standing around the back of the room, leaning against the walls. Don and I could not believe that so many people were coming. But one thing we did believe, along with the original ten or fifteen people, was that when we prayed, God answered. And when we prayed for San Diego, God brought unbelievers to attend the Bible studies and give their lives to Jesus.

Prayer in Linda Vista

Just eight months after the beginning of the Monday night Bible study, we had outgrown the living room of a house and the five hundred seats of an old auditorium. We relocated about seven miles away to the north where we found an old Baptist church building that was empty. We didn't have any money other than a few dollars from the offering to pay rent, so we took on a month-to-month lease at ten cents per square foot. We thought that was a lot of money. How could God ever provide that much for us each month? Could we survive?

The first thing we did was assemble the original group for prayer: God brought the new people. We were now filling the 750 seats of this run-down old church facility. One year to the day after we started, we had a Monday night Bible study and Sunday morning and Sunday night studies

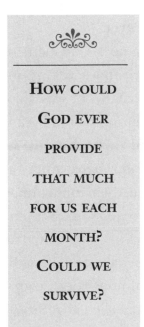

HOW COULD

GOD EVER

PROVIDE

THAT MUCH

FOR US EACH

MONTH?

COULD WE

SURVIVE?

going—with praycr meetings before, during, and after each service. Plus, the people were gathering in their apartments and homes to pray together for this new and fresh work of the Holy Spirit. Prayer literally launched a worldwide ministry in San Diego!

Prayer in North Park Theater

Corrie ten Boom was a godly woman and a true saint. If you have never read her book *The Hiding Place* or seen a movie, video, or DVD of it, you need to get a copy and enjoy the story of a woman who truly knew Jesus. Her father owned a clock shop in Haarlem, a community near Amsterdam, Holland. During the Second World War, Corrie's mother and father felt compassion for the persecuted Jewish people of their country. They actually hid Jews in their home above the clock shop until they could escape to a neutral country and be safe from German authorities.

As the book tells us, the activities of Corrie's family were discovered, and the Nazis imprisoned Corrie and her sister. It was during these terrible times of her life that Corrie learned to live a life of faith, a life of Bible study, and a life of prayer.

Corrie was an elderly woman when I became a Christian in 1970. However, she was still sharing her faith and speaking in churches wherever and whenever she had the chance. I was able to hear her speak, and to say that she was inspiring would be an understatement. When her book was released in bookstores, it became an immediate best-seller. Following her book came a movie of the courageous Ten Boom family and their miraculous encounters with God during the German occupation of their Dutch homeland.

One evening in 1975, Sandy and I went to see this movie with another couple in San Diego. The theater was in an older neighborhood of town, and the building was simply called the North

Park Theater. This neighborhood (called North Park) was on the northern end of Balboa Park. The homes in the immediate vicinity of the theater and the commercial section were built from the 1920s to the 1940s.

The theater had quite a history. It was built in 1929 for live theater and vaudeville acts. The ceilings were high, with chandeliers hanging from them. It had beautiful hand-carved moldings wrapping around the walls, high-back leather seats in the loge section, and a pervading sense of a bygone era. It was run-down and in need of repair, but it had a beautiful ambience to it.

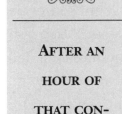

AFTER AN HOUR OF THAT CONTINUAL QUESTION, SANDY SAID, "BE QUIET AND WATCH THE MOVIE."

While watching the much-anticipated release of *The Hiding Place*, I kept turning to Sandy and our friends throughout the night, saying, "Wouldn't this be a great church?"

Finally, after an hour of that continual question, Sandy said, "Be quiet and watch the movie."

Little did I know that the Holy Spirit was at work in my heart that night. He was inspiring my faith through the context of the movie, and he was stirring my faith inside of an old theater.

One month later, out of the blue I received a telephone call from a real estate broker. He had heard that we were a growing church without a home and that our current building was too small for us. Little did he know that we had consistently been praying for God to give us a larger home.

"Would you be interested in an old movie theater?" he asked me.

"Yes, we would. How many people does it seat, and where is it located?"

He talked about an old theater that seated about 1,250 people and was called the North Park Theater! The realtor said that he would be happy to walk me through the building if I wanted to see it. Who could have ever imagined such a thing? Well, I can tell you that God *could* imagine it—and, in fact, he *did* imagine it.

The next nine years of ministry would be profound for San Diego. The power of prayer was unleashed in prayer meetings in the theater, in home fellowship groups throughout the county, and at the workplaces of many people. Prayer breakfast meetings were held every week in the back rooms of restaurants in every part of the county. In that period, about one new church each year was launched from the pastoral staff and by gathering home fellowships in the different zip code areas of the city and county.

Even the purchase of the building was the fruit of prayer. Our church was too new for a bank to lend us money, so we had to trust God—and God worked in a mysterious way. I seldom have seen rich people with excess cash come to the aid of the work of the Lord; but several times I have seen him use the poor and working class to accomplish miracles.

In this case, it was a young widow whose husband had died in the crash of a private airplane. She took some of the insurance benefits and used them to guarantee a loan for the church. After we had been making payments for about six years, God used another widow who donated the money to pay off the bank loan through a tithe of her deceased husband's estate. Prayer did what banks could not do.

After nine years in a facility that had seen the salvation of thousands of people, without having even one parking space, it was time to move. Our church had quickly become the largest congregation in San Diego. Remember, it had grown from a small group of only ten people. But these ten people, and the tens of thousands who followed them, were praying people.

Growth through Prayer

Where could we find property for such a large congregation when we really didn't place a lot of emphasis on money or the material aspects of the ministry? We were focused on our simple three-step vision: (1) win a person *to* Jesus Christ; (2) disciple that person *in* Jesus Christ; and (3) send that person out to witness *for* Jesus Christ.

We were, and hopefully have always been, a people-oriented ministry. Again God would show himself faithful by directing us to a twenty-two-acre junior high school that was empty and that we could lease for twenty years. Who would have thought that we would launch one church approximately every twelve months, send missionaries all around the world, establish evangelistic outreaches to win thousands to God's kingdom, start a preschool and an elementary school, train dozens of people to become pastors—and do it all in a space of 20,000 square feet without one parking space? Only God could have figured that one out—we sure didn't!

The answer to our prayers came in an explosion of growth. We went from 20,000 square feet of land to 22 acres of land with enough parking for 500 cars. This startling growth has taught me to be careful what I ask for when I pray, because I might get it. Also, it may be more than I ask for.

Prayer in Clairemont

God is so good to us that we often forget how good he really is. We prayed for a new facility, but we didn't pray or plan for growth of the congregation or the funds to cover the physical growth of the facility. For example, our water bill went from $100 per month to $1,000 per month. Our electricity bill went from $1,000 per month to $10,000 per month immediately (though in recent years, with the energy crunch, our electricity bill has risen to $36,000 per month). Yet for the past eighteen years at this facility we have never missed one electricity or water payment. We have also never failed to meet the need for $1,000 per month to pay for the fertilizer necessary to cover all the lawns and gardens on the campus!

Now we are at the end of our twenty-year lease, and we have more than a hundred churches and parachurch ministries that have grown from this facility. That is almost one new work every six months. Prayer is still our focus and a must for us, because now property rates are at $1.3 million per acre in San Diego. We now have the largest private school in San Diego and lease two campuses from the local school district. If we were to combine the church and the preschool, elementary, junior high, and senior high schools onto one campus, it would cost close to $50 million to buy thirty-five acres and build new facilities.

Will I say, "No way. We can't do it"? Of course I won't, because we have been praying and continue to pray for a new facility and for God's perfect will. Basically, we are a debt-free ministry just as my pastor taught me. Since I am entering what are probably the last twenty years of my pastorate, I have no desire to leave a congregation with debt. I am convinced that God will provide again.

Prayer in Downtown San Diego

Within a ten-mile radius of our church facility, there are eight congregations that have grown from our original body of believers. All of the pastors and many of their staff members were at one time members of this great praying church. It is estimated that they represent approximately 10,000 people worshiping God in San Diego on any Sunday morning. That is only a third of the churches in the county that have come out of the original work in 1974 with ten people and which are either first- or second-generation works.

I hope you can see that prayer launched a wonderful ministry to one of America's finest cities. Hopefully you can also see that God's building blocks in your life are raising you up to a new level. If you can grasp that fact, falling in love with prayer will open doors of opportunity for you and your family. If you will commit yourself to becoming a person of prayer, you can grow personally and can be used to launch a new, dynamic spiritual life.

> FALLING IN LOVE WITH PRAYER WILL OPEN DOORS OF OPPORTUNITY FOR YOU AND YOUR FAMILY.

At Jesus' Word

There is a story in the New Testament that is filled with powerful metaphor. This story about Jesus leaves our minds open to a great deal of imagination and provides marvelous insight into our own futures.

> *So it was, as the multitude pressed about Him to hear the word of God, that He stood by the Lake of Gennesaret, and saw two boats standing by the lake; but the fishermen had gone from them and were washing their nets. Then He got into one of the boats, which was Simon's, and asked him to put out a little from the land. And He sat down and taught the multitudes from the boat.*
>
> *Now when He had stopped speaking, He said to Simon, "Launch out into the deep and let down your nets for a catch." But Simon answered and said to Him,*

"Master, we have toiled all night and caught nothing;
nevertheless at Your word I will let down the net." And
when they had done this, they caught a great number of
fish, and their net was breaking. So they signaled to their
partners in the other boat to come and help them. And
they came and filled both the boats, so that they began to
sink (Luke 5:1–7 NKJV).

What a classic picture for us to develop in our hearts and minds. Jesus was about His Father's business, teaching people about the kingdom of God. The crowds had grown to a point that Jesus was apparently pushed to the shoreline of the Sea of Galilee (which was also known as the Lake of Gennesaret, the Sea of Tiberias, and in the Old Testament the Sea of Chinnereth).

If you have never been to Israel, let me assure you that the word *sea* is a good description because the term *lake* may conjure up in your mind a small body of water. This lake is twelve and a half miles long, and from four to seven and a half miles wide. It is situated 682 feet below the level of the Mediterranean, and is between 80 and 160 feet deep.

I can identify with Jesus' wanting to get into a boat and be off shore while talking to the people. For almost thirty years, we have baptized people in Mission Bay. This beautiful bay is renowned to the people of San Diego. For the past twenty-nine years, somewhere between 150 and 350 people have been baptized at a time in the salty water of the bay. It is a wonderful time to see God at work in our city, because hundreds of people who have been baptized or are friends and family of those being baptized join in the event.

Usually, this mass baptism occurs around dinnertime, so everyone is cooking on their barbecue grills or playing softball or throwing Frisbees®. Many are playing guitars and singing. It probably is much like the festive atmosphere when the multitudes came to Jesus. However, when it is time to begin the baptism, everyone comes to the edge of the sand and leaves the grassy areas of the park. We all pray and worship together. Then I stand, with hundreds sitting around me, and explain the biblical perspective of water baptism. About twenty or thirty pastors and home fellowship leaders and elders form a very wide line in the knee-deep water behind me.

Every year we give an invitation for salvation, and many people who came to observe or who "just happened" to be at the beach pray to receive Jesus Christ as their Lord and Savior. One of my last admonitions to the crowds is always to wait at the edge of the water until they see one of the ministers available to baptize them. Then they should enter the water and walk out to the minister. The reason is simple: When there are a couple of hundred people wanting to be baptized, and they all walk into the water at once, the ministers have to keep backing up into deeper water.

Jesus needed to be distanced from the people to meet their needs, so he chose a small boat that belonged to Simon (or Peter, as he is also called), and that little fishing craft became his "pulpit." When he was finished preaching, he showed how gracious he is. It is a great lesson to remember about sharing by giving what we have to the Lord.

Luke tells that Jesus said to Simon, "Launch out into the deep and let down your nets for a catch" (Luke 5:4 NKJV). Jesus wanted to repay Simon Peter for the use of his business tool, and he knew that Simon needed to go deeper to be rewarded. But Simon answered and said to him, "Master, we have toiled all night and caught nothing; nevertheless at Your word I will let down the net" (Luke 5:5 NKJV).

Peter was resistant to this suggestion of Jesus. He, after all, was the fisherman, and Jesus was the preaching carpenter. Peter reminded him that he and his partners had worked all night and had caught nothing. How like you and me that is. We too go about our daily affairs and regular business, and many times come home empty and tired and discouraged. We, like Simon, have toiled and are exhausted from our own efforts.

The redeeming feature is that Peter's response included the words "nevertheless *at Your word*" (v. 5). The word of the Lord is

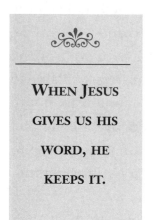

WHEN JESUS GIVES US HIS WORD, HE KEEPS IT.

what we want to direct our lives and our daily affairs. The word of Jesus had been very fruitful in the eyes of Peter, and he would respect the carpenter one more time and do as he said. When Peter and his partners had done what Jesus told them to do, they caught a great number of fish, so many that their net began to break (see v. 6).

This is a lesson we all need to learn and remember. When Jesus gives us his word, he keeps it. The same is true with us and our prayer lives. When we ask of him, we need to be prepared to receive from him—many times much more than we have asked for.

When we fall in love with prayer, we become like Simon Peter. We don't always understand what is going on, but we know who will handle the situation for us. When we are dog tired and discouraged from struggling with our circumstances, we can simply pray and seek the Lord and his goodness.

Catch the Vision

Over the years, in our ministry we have seen the Holy Spirit give vision to many, many people. As you know, Proverbs 29:18 says,

"Where there is no vision, the people perish" (KJV). That verse has been illuminated time and again in our ministry. It seems that when there is a congregation that is totally committed to the Word of God, and when prayer is also an integral part of that congregation, God reveals the future to his people. He reveals through a vision his plan for them. With prayer and in-depth Bible study, vision comes to the hearts of God's people.

It is not good for spiritual leaders to have a vision for God's people and keep it to themselves. It is also not good for a spiritual leader to use the people to fulfill his or her own personal vision. A vision should be used to build the body of Christ.

We have all seen preachers on television who claim to have received a vision from God. Whatever their individual vision may be, it usually has to do with money. Many times they want us to sow into their ministry so that they can fulfill the vision that God has given them.

That isn't the kind of vision that I am referring to here. Prayer brings clarity of vision for each of us. Prayer opens our communication channels with God. Prayer reveals to us the deeper meaning of Scripture. Prayer keeps us in line with the plans and purposes of God. When more people pray and receive vision, the church of our Lord and Savior Jesus Christ grows. This is the type of prayer that has launched one of the greatest churches in history. (Of course, I may be just a little prejudiced in my viewpoint of this subject!)

Many times over the years I have received letters, cards, and emails saying, "We are praying for you, Mike," or, "We are praying for you and your family." I am humbled that so many people would spend even one second in prayer for me and my family. I know that it is these prayers that have helped us through painful situations, financial hardships, and disappointing setbacks. These prayers have brought to our family many of the blessings we enjoy today.

Launch Out!

As you can see, prayer launched our ministry in San Diego. The early building blocks in my spiritual walk with the Lord set the stage. Hopefully, after reading this account your faith will increase, and you will accept the notion that prayer will launch your ministry or your family or your relationship with God.

When we think of the huge rockets that lift the space shuttle off the launching pad at Cape Kennedy, it can be mind-boggling. Those massive engines have tremendous thrust and can launch just about anything into space. When they run out of rocket fuel though, it is another story. The rockets fall off and drop down thousands of feet into the Atlantic Ocean, to be picked up by U.S. Navy vessels.

However, when we launch into prayer, we need no special astronaut training courses, no special space suits, no special clearance from NASA or the FAA. When we launch out toward heaven in prayer, our boosters don't fall off. Nor do we run out of fuel. God receives our prayers in an instant and responds to them in his own wisdom and way.

Take note of the conversation between Daniel the prophet and Gabriel the angel:

> *While I was speaking in prayer, the man Gabriel, whom I had seen in the vision at the beginning, being caused to fly swiftly, reached me about the time of the evening offering. And he informed me, and talked with me, and said, "O Daniel, I have now come forth to give you skill to understand.*

"At the beginning of your supplications the command went out, and I have come to tell you, for you are greatly beloved; therefore consider the matter, and understand the vision" (Dan. 9:21–23 NKJV, *emphasis added*).

While Daniel was speaking in prayer, God commanded Gabriel to go down to earth and encourage Daniel and give him understanding of the vision. When you pray, remember that God is listening, and he is ready to launch you with encouragement from heaven.

Fall in Love with Prayer

When you remember that our church is only one of about 1,250 in the San Diego area, it seems obvious that God has a lot of people in that city to work with and through. Please do not think that I am saying we are the only spiritual work or the only church

REMEMBER THAT GOD IS LISTENING, AND HE IS READY TO LAUNCH YOU WITH ENCOURAGEMENT FROM HEAVEN.

doing anything for and through God. We are absolutely not. We are only one church that loves God, seeks God, and serves God. But we are a group of believers whom God has launched into the deep of our city. God has allowed himself to be glorified through our small segment of his people.

Today orphanages, youth ministries, churches, schools, publishing and recording ministries, benevolent ministries for the poor, Bible and evangelism schools, evangelistic outreaches, home fellowships, and prayer teams have spread throughout the earth from our church—simply because the first ten people launched into prayer for their original group and for the lost people of San Diego. Then every subsequent group has continued this calling to pray and seek God's vision for their lives. May God's blessings be poured out upon you, and may you fall in love with prayer!

CHAPTER SIX

OUR PRAYERS ON THE ALTAR

"Prayer is a shield to the soul, a sacrifice to God,
and a scourge for Satan."
JOHN BUNYAN

Altars do not have a significant place in our culture. We may talk about brides and grooms "going to the altar," and we may hear a pastor encourage parishioners to bring their "tithes and offerings to the altar of the Lord."

But for the most part, people in our society view altars as relics from antiquity—something from the olden days with no relevance in our "enlightened" era. That's too bad, because the Bible is full of references to altars—the actual kind made of stones, and the symbolic kind that represents an attitude of the heart.

In this chapter, we are going to explore prayer in the context of altars, those sacred places where sacrifices are made and meetings with the Lord take place. Specifically, we will examine the life of Abraham and his experience with altars. As we do, we will find significant truths for our own prayer lives.

God Calls Abraham

We pick up the story of Abraham while he was still called Abram, before God gave him a name change:

> *The LORD had said to Abram, "Leave your country,*
> *your people and your father's household and go the land I*
> *will show you. I will make you into a great nation and I*
> *will bless you; I will make your name great, and you will be*
> *a blessing. I will bless those who bless you, and whoever*
> *curses you I will curse; and all peoples on earth will be*
> *blessed through you."*
> *So Abram left, as the LORD had told him; and Lot*
> *went with him. Abram was seventy-five years old when he*
> *set out from Haran (Gen. 12:1–4).*

It is easy to skip over the fact that Abram sinned. God had told him to leave behind all of his family, but he took his nephew Lot along, and this nephew eventually became a problem to him.

Abram journeyed from his homeland to a place called Canaan. When he got there, the Lord appeared to him and told him that his descendants would inherit the land.

> *So he built an altar there to the LORD, who had*
> *appeared to him. From there he went on toward the hills*
> *east of Bethel and pitched his tent, with Bethel on the west*
> *and Ai on the east. There he built an altar to the LORD*
> *and called on the name of the LORD. Then Abram set out*
> *and continued toward the Negev (Gen. 12:7–9).*

Abram built an altar and "called on the name of the LORD" (v. 8), which is another way of saying that he prayed. After Abram went up from Egypt, he went on his journey from the south until he came to Bethel, where he had built an altar, and again "Abram called on the name of the LORD" (Gen. 13:4). A few verses later, we learn that "Abram moved his tent, and went and dwelt by the terebinth trees of Mamre, which are in Hebron, and built an altar there to the LORD" (Gen. 13:18 NKJV).

Abram was obviously a man of the altar. It is interesting to note that in those days pagans had altars too, and they offered sacrifices to their gods on them. The Canaanites in the Promised Land were worshipers of pagan gods, which is why God later told his people, the children of Israel, "Wipe them out, them and their altars; this is going to be my land, and I want it to be pure" (see Exod. 23:20–26). That is also why Abram built his own altar, because he wanted to worship the Lord on a fresh, clean altar—not on another man's altar, and not on one that had been polluted by evil practices.

> THERE IS NO PLACE LIKE THE ALTAR OF PRAYER TO FIND DIRECTION AND COUNSEL FROM GOD.

That should be a lesson for you and me. We should realize how important it is for us to have a clean, untainted altar constructed with our own hands, a pure place to meet the Lord. One that nobody else has built, but one that we have built with our worship, prayer, and praise, in order to lift up the name of the Lord.

According to *Vine's Complete Expository Dictionary*, the word *altar* means "slaughter place." (Vine 1996) That's why it was always a place of sacrifice. For us, prayer involves sacrifice. It is a sacrifice of our time, our effort, and our energy. We lay ourselves on the altar, saying, "God, this is what's going on in my life. I feel so depressed and discouraged I don't know what to do. I give my life to you, Lord, and I trust you to take it and make something wonderful out of it." The apostle

Paul emphasized this theme of sacrifice in his letter to the Romans: "I urge you, brothers, in view of God's mercy, to offer your bodies as living sacrifices, holy and pleasing to God—this is your spiritual act of worship" (Rom. 12:1). We become the sacrifice on this beautiful altar that we ourselves have built, and it gets bigger and stronger every day as we offer our life and our prayers to the Lord on it.

Abraham received many blessings and benefits as he built altars, or places on which to worship and communicate with God. These same blessings can be ours as we follow Abraham's example:

Guidance. In order to fulfill his commission, Abraham needed guidance. There is no place like the altar of prayer to find direction and counsel from God. As we read in Proverbs 14:12, "There is a way that seems right to a man, but in the end it leads to death." So often we struggle to know the right path to take: *Is God calling me to go this way or that way? Is he telling me to take this job or go back to school? Is he leading me to take the road on the left or the one on the right? If I go straight ahead, am I going to run into trouble?* At the altar where we meet God, we receive his direction.

Comfort. We all need comfort now and then, and what better place to find it than in prayer? When we sit alone, quietly communing with the Lord, his peace comes to us, and we know that God has touched us. Wherever Abraham had a tent, God had an altar. Wherever Abraham settled down, God had a place to be worshiped. We receive his soothing touch when we meet with him in our private, sacred place.

Strength. Abraham was going to fight some difficult battles; he was going into some hostile territory. He was going to see his nephew get caught up with some bad people. He was going to have to send three hundred trained servants into battles against kings and mighty armies. He was going to need tremendous strength to put up with continual harassment.

We may cry out, "God, I can't confront this situation. I'm just too weak. I'm in way over my head." In such times God gives us strength because he has called us to complete a mission. We may say, "What you're calling me to do makes no sense, Lord. I don't have what it takes to accomplish it." It may not make sense from a human perspective, but if we will trust him to do so, God will give us the extra strength we need to do whatever he has called us to do.

Courage. Abraham needed courage to fulfill his commission, and so do you and I. We need boldness and bravery to live godly lives, to stand up for truth and righteousness. We need courage to face the evil that creeps down our streets every day and tries to sneak into our homes. As Jeremiah said to the people of Israel when the nation fell apart, "Death has climbed in through our windows and has entered our fortresses" (Jer. 9:21). We need supernatural courage to fend off temptation and immorality. Go to God in prayer, and he will give you that courage. Seek the Lord, and he will provide what you need to face life and all of its hardships and challenges.

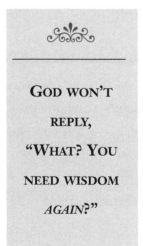

GOD WON'T REPLY, "WHAT? YOU NEED WISDOM AGAIN?"

Wisdom. Like Abraham, we need wisdom to keep away from many of the things this world offers us that might confuse us. I love what James wrote: "But the wisdom that comes from heaven is first of all pure; then peace-loving, considerate, submissive, full of mercy and good fruit, impartial and sincere" (James 3:17). James also wrote, "If any of you lacks wisdom, he should ask of God, who gives generously to all without finding fault, and it will be given to him" (James 1:5).

God will not get upset if you say, "Lord, I need wisdom." He won't reply, "What? You need wisdom *again*? You should know better by now!" You may have grown up in a family in which you were ridiculed or even punished for asking "dumb questions." You may have been shamed for not knowing the answers to all of life's dilemmas. God won't treat you that way. He has promised to give you wisdom, and the way you receive it is through prayer.

Waiting on God

In Genesis 15, Abraham was concerned because he didn't have an heir. God had promised that his descendants would become a great nation, but he had no children.

> *After this, the word of the LORD came to Abram in a vision: "Do not be afraid, Abram. I am your shield, your very great reward." But Abram said, "O Sovereign LORD, what can you give me since I remain childless and the one who will inherit my estate is Eliezer of Damascus?" (Gen. 15:1–2).*

Abraham learned that *God's delays are not God's denials.* It was twenty-five years earlier that Abraham had received the promise (see Gen. 12:1–3). Two and a half decades had gone by, and the prayer had not been answered. (We often get frustrated when God doesn't answer us in a few days or weeks!)

We should not interpret Abraham's response to God as doubt or skepticism. Abraham was just raising up his prayer again: "Lord,

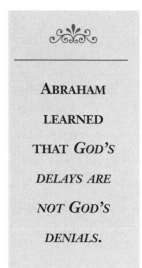

ABRAHAM LEARNED THAT *GOD'S DELAYS ARE NOT GOD'S DENIALS.*

I remember your promise, and I know you will deliver. But, you see, at the moment I still have no heir."

Abraham believed God. We are told in verse 6 of Genesis 15, "Abraham believed the LORD, and he credited it to him as right-eousness." We learn from Abraham that what God has promised, he will fulfill in his own time (see Rom. 4:20–21). We should never give up on prayer.

To me, the altar of prayer is like a resting place. Not only a resting place to catch my breath and seek God, but a resting place for prayer issues. God often answers prayers in his own way, in his own time. Our job is to maintain faith that he will come through. In fact, this biblical principle became a cornerstone of my early Christian foundation. As Hebrews 11:6 tells us, "Without faith it is impossible to please him: for he that cometh to God must believe that he is, and that he is a rewarder of them that diligently seek him" (KJV).

When we place something upon the altar, we must leave it there for God to receive the sweet-smelling savor of it (see Eph. 5:2 KJV). I have found that in seeking God's will, it is as if a priest walks up to the altar in the temple and lays down a sacrifice before God. It is the same with the prayers that I lift up to him by placing them on his altar—I must leave them there and wait for the Lord to act according to his will.

The Cry of the Heart

Sarai, Abram's wife, had borne him no children, so she gave her Egyptian handmaiden, Hagar, to her husband: "[Sarai] said to

Abram, 'The LORD has kept me from having children. Go, sleep with my maidservant; perhaps I can build a family through her'" (Gen. 16:2).

So, of course, he said yes. With Sarai's permission, he committed adultery, and Hagar became pregnant. "When she knew she was pregnant, she began to despise her mistress" (Gen. 16:4). Sarai became envious and complained to Abram about Hagar's attitude toward her. Abram told Sarai to do with Hagar whatever she wanted: "Then Sarai mistreated Hagar; so she fled from her" (Gen. 16:6). Hagar went out into the desert, where the angel of the Lord found her near a spring:

> *Then the angel of the LORD told her, "Go back to your mistress and submit to her." The angel added, "I will so increase your descendants that they will be too numerous to count." The angel of the LORD also said to her: "You are now with child and you will have a son. You shall name him Ishmael, for the LORD has heard of your misery"* (Gen. 16: 9–11).

The Lord hears our misery. We can see and feel affliction, but only the Lord can hear it. If you have deep pain in your heart, God hears your cries and your groaning (see Acts 7:34). Your closest friends can see it, you can feel it, but God can hear it churning inside of you.

Think of the angel's words: "Go back to your mistress." It is very hard for us to go back to where our trouble started. It is hard to return to the place where we were unwanted or unappreciated, or where we were misunderstood and mistreated. But in order for Hagar to receive the promised blessing of the Lord, the angel told her to "go back."

You may cringe at the thought of going back to the source of your pain, of returning to the place and the people that caused your misery. You may have to humble yourself in the sight of those people. The Lord is going to bless you there, for he has heard your cries and your groaning of despair.

IF YOU ARE EXPERIENCING PAIN IN YOUR SOUL, TAKE IT TO GOD.

In such a trying time as this, Hagar's painful experience was where she met God. Pain is often used by God to draw us to himself. It was in this ugly, dark, deep pit of affliction that Hagar heard a direct message from the Lord. It seemed hard for her to return to the place from which she had just fled, but in obeying God's voice she eventually found rest and joy.

Hagar's tough times gave birth to one of the most comforting phrases in the Bible: "You are the God who sees me" (Gen. 16:13). Tough times remind us that God answers prayer and that his eyes are upon us. It is possible that Hagar would never have known God if she had not experienced that anguish of soul.

If you are experiencing pain in your soul, take it to God. You may be facing a marital crisis, even divorce. You may have been unemployed for months. You may be having all kinds of problems with your children. This is a word of encouragement to you: In the midst of your pain, you can meet God in a whole new way. He has heard your affliction, and he sees you.

Dr. John Walvoord, the former president of Dallas Theological Seminary, once said, "Prayer is much like a check to be countersigned by two parties. I sign the check and I send it up to heaven, and if Jesus Christ also signs it, it does not matter how large it is, it will be honored." Start sending your prayers to heaven.

Trust and Obey

The Old Testament is filled with examples of God speaking to human beings—of people crying out to him, and the Lord responding. Commands were given, promises were made, and the early saints simply believed God's promises and followed the instructions he gave them.

In our era of cynicism and skepticism, we are tempted to doubt God's promises. We sometimes fail to take God at his word. In Old Testament times, believers, for the most part, trusted God as the sovereign ruler of heaven and earth. Not that this was always easy. In fact, this trust was sometimes put to the test.

According to the covenant God made with Abraham, he did eventually give him an heir through his wife Sarai (later called Sarah). But then God did something that would have shaken the faith of lesser men:

> Some time later God tested Abraham. He said to him, "Abraham!"
>
> "Here I am," he replied.
>
> Then God said, "Take your son, your only son, Isaac, whom you love, and go to the region of Moriah. Sacrifice him there as a burnt offering on one of the mountains I will tell you about" (Gen. 22:1–2).

Note the silence of Abraham when God commanded him to offer up his son as a sacrifice. God had been allowing Abraham to build altars all along, and he had worshiped God at them. Every time Abraham moved, he built an altar so he could commune with the Lord. But then God issued an unusual command: "Build another altar and put your son on it and offer him to me." We can be sure that Abraham had strong feelings about this directive, but we should also note that there was no arguing, no questioning, no doubting. God spoke to him, so he obeyed—it was that simple.

If you have children, you know the anguish that comes to your heart when they are in danger. I know I do. Our youngest son, Phillip, had terrible battles with croup when he was young. One night when he was about three years old, his throat began to close, and he had great difficulty breathing. Obviously, his mother and I were extremely concerned. We tried using the vaporizer and other remedies, but nothing worked. His breathing became much more labored, and I began to fear the worst.

I told Sandy to keep praying as I ran to the car with Phillip in my arms. I raced off toward the emergency room at our local hospital. It was normally a ten- or fifteen-minute drive, but that night it took only five minutes.

Rushing into the ER, I begged the nurses to help me as fast as they could. They immediately paged the on-call doctor and put Phillip on a gurney. They gave him a shot and waited awhile. When his breathing did not improve, they gave him a second shot. Still no improvement.

Then they put him on an inhaler and gave him oxygen. None of this brought the relief that our little guy needed. Watching him struggle was a heart-wrenching experience for me.

Finally, the doctor told me that Phillip needed specialty care and that we should immediately go to Children's Hospital, about twenty miles away. The doctor said that time was of the essence and that I could drive there faster than it would take an ambulance to get to the hospital and transport him. It was a true emergency, one that hung on the edge of life or death.

Again I took Phillip's limp little body and bolted down the freeway. The thirty-minute drive was completed in about twenty minutes. When the medical personnel took Phillip from me and asked me to fill out the required papers and wait, I remembered the story of Abraham offering Isaac on the altar to God. When Abraham took Isaac up the hill, he turned and said to his servants, "The boy and I will return" (see Gen. 2:3–5).

By faith I "laid Phillip on the altar," knowing that my son and I would return. He was medicated and placed inside an oxygen tent. I curled up on the floor next to him and prayed through the night, sleeping and praying, sleeping and praying.

PRAYER IS WALKING AND TALKING TOGETHER WITH GOD.

My prayers, along with the excellent medical care, worked. The next day, Phillip was released, and we went home to see his mom and his four siblings. The boy and I did indeed return.

Laying a child on the altar is a difficult thing to do. But Abraham's life was an example to me to keep my trust in God.

Fall in Love with Prayer

Prayer is communication. It is walking and talking together with God. Prayer is connected to habitual spiritual growth with the Lord. Prayer is also an altar of sacrifice. It is the place where we meet God and lay ourselves down before him in total honesty with him. In prayer we empty ourselves like a sacrificial lamb lying on the altar with all of its blood draining out. When we lay our heart before God on his altar, he accepts it as our sacrifice.

We know that prayer, whether filled with joy or anguish, is heard by God. When pain comes, it is not a time to run away or to take refuge in drink or drugs. It is not a time to scurry about seeking a short-term, feel-good remedy. It is a time to get on our knees and face God. In our pain and anguish God hears our affliction.

When he hears our cry, he will come down from heaven and take us back where we belong. *He* will straighten everything out.

Lay your prayers on the altar. Lay yourself on the altar. God will lovingly receive your sacrifice and respond with compassion.

CHAPTER SEVEN

THE POWER OF PRAYING TOGETHER

"Pray as if everything depended upon your prayer."
WILLIAM BOOTH

It was a balmy summer night in San Diego, and I was riding along with a police officer from the Eastern Division. This particular evening, there was a planned sweep through an area known for its street prostitutes.

One of our first arrests was a twenty-year-old Jennifer Lopez look-alike, and we drove to police headquarters downtown to book her. Then we would take her to Las Colinas, a women's detention center in East County, about forty-five minutes away.

While the officer went in to begin the booking process, I sat quietly in the front passenger seat, with the young woman, Angela, behind me in the back seat. Her hands were cuffed, and there was a screen mesh between the two of us. After a few minutes of silence, I told her that I would like to ask a question, if it was okay with her. I explained that I was not a cop but a police chaplain, and that nothing we talked about would be used against her in a legal way. She said that was fine.

"You seem to be bright and attractive," I said. "So what motivates you to walk the streets?"

Angela was not offended by the question and stated that she could understand why I would ask it. She explained that she was a high school dropout. Her mother and father disowned her when she became pregnant at the age of fifteen. The boyfriend who had "loved" her denied that it was his baby and wanted nothing to do with her. So she was on the streets to make money to buy food and pay the bills. This is how she had been earning a living for the past four years, ever since her baby was born.

She wasn't afraid of getting AIDS or of being beaten up by a stranger or of having a police record. Her friends did not know she was a prostitute. In fact, they thought she was a single mom who had lost her husband in an accident and was living off the insurance money and attending college at night.

She made a lot of money in the sex industry and had to work only a few nights each month. She explained to me that one night would pay the month's rent, two nights would pay the car expense, and three nights covered food and all her necessities. That night she was going to be out for only a few hours because she wanted to purchase a table and chairs for her dining room. When special things came up that she wanted to buy, she would go to the streets and get the money.

Angela lived in a town south of San Diego, toward the Tijuana, Mexico, border. So this street, where she regularly worked, was far enough away from her home and neighborhood that she wouldn't be spotted by anyone she knew. She had lived a secret life for the past four years and was at peace with it—or so she said. She loved her son and had provided a nice apartment for the two of them, bought her own car, and was able to dress nicely.

After she finished talking, the police officer came out of the booking office and began walking across the parking lot toward us. Not wanting to embarrass her in front of the officer, I asked quickly, "Do you know God?"

She said no. She knew nothing about him and really wasn't interested. But she appreciated my asking.

The long drive to the women's detention center was quiet except for the chatter of the radio and the small talk between the officer and me. When we parked at the detention center, the officer told me to stand by the back door of the car. He would go inside and lock his pistol in a gun safe. Then he would wave to me to bring the prisoner in. There were about five other women in line to be handed over to the jailer, and once they were processed, he motioned for me to bring Angela to the entry door.

When she got out of the car and stood up, she looked at me and said, "Chaplain, would you please remember to pray for me and for my soul and my son? I lied to you about not knowing God. When I was a young girl, I always prayed and went to church and read the Bible. When I was eleven years old, I told my mother that when I grew up I wanted to be a nun."

WHAT KIND OF A MOTHER COULD SAY SUCH A THING TO HER DAUGHTER?

Her mother's response to this young, sweet, and sensitive preadolescent was, "God wouldn't want a bad girl like you."

Memories of that evening, that arrest, that young woman, and that statement from her mother have bounced around inside my head for years. I have continued to pray for Angela and her son.

Churches Need to Grow in Prayer

As you were reading that story, you probably had the same reaction I had at the time:

What kind of a mother could say such a thing to her daughter? No wonder that young woman went on to make terrible choices. And why wouldn't God want a "bad girl"? Is it only good people who can join his family and become useful members of his church?

Today there is a vast misunderstanding about what church is, what it means to be a Christian, and what kind of people God wants. Angela's mother obviously did not understand what church was about. Apparently, Angela knew that God had spoken to her in church, and she wanted to respond to him at an early age. However, her mother seemed to have the mistaken idea that little girls who were a problem to their parents definitely would be a problem to God. Nothing could be further from the truth. That eleven year old wasn't a little girl for long, because four years later she found herself pregnant.

I wonder whether that mother would have treated her child differently if she had been in a church that taught people to pray to a loving, compassionate, gracious God. Prayer could have opened her eyes to the understanding that God was calling her child, just as he called young Jeremiah in the Bible:

> *The word of the LORD came to me, saying: "Before I formed you in the womb I knew you, before you were born I set you apart; I appointed you as a prophet to the nations."*
>
> *"Ah, Sovereign LORD," I said. I do not know how to speak; I am only a child."*
>
> *But the LORD said to me, "Do not say, 'I am only a child.' You must go to everyone I send you to and say whatever I command you. Do not be afraid of them, for I am with you and will rescue you," declares the LORD (Jer. 1:4–8).*

God calls people of all ages to come to him. It is the church's responsibility to nurture their spiritual growth and maturity. But, you may ask, what is a church? Usually, the word *church* calls to our mind images of steeples and spires, pews and altars, crosses and stained-glass windows. As you travel through Europe and Great Britain, these massive structures of stone definitely do speak of an era gone by—a time when masons, carpenters, and craftsmen were busy designing and building edifices "to the glory of God." Today, in a post-Christian era, a large number of these outdated designs are museums, mosques, bars, and dance clubs.

I remember preaching one Sunday morning in Edinburgh, Scotland. That church building had high ceilings and stone walls and floors, which did little to keep out the frigid wintry air. Since it was nearly as cold inside as it was outside, every parishioner wore a coat and scarf. Some of the older ladies had on full-length fur coats. The choir stood in the loft singing old hymns from books published at least a hundred years ago, and each choir member wore a coat, mittens, and scarf. I think one or two may have been wearing earmuffs.

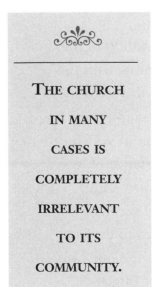

THE CHURCH IN MANY CASES IS COMPLETELY IRRELEVANT TO ITS COMMUNITY.

I thought to myself, *What teenager or young couple would want to get up early on Sunday morning and come into an old museum like this to freeze while singing outdated songs they don't know?*

My point is that the church in many cases is completely irrelevant to its community. Many churches are outmoded and outdated, not just in regard to architecture and facilities, but also in mission and in reflection of the God who loves all of us so much that he sent his only begotten Son down to earth to redeem us from our sins.

A Collection of Believers

A church is not a building; it is a group of people who believe in the lordship of Jesus Christ. These people have exercised their faith to believe what Jesus said in the Gospel of John: "For God so loved the world that He gave His one and only Son, that whoever believes in Him should not perish but have eternal life" (John 3:16).

Somewhere between the first century and the twenty-first century, the word *church* has lost its real meaning and has taken on an essence that keeps people from knowing God. Read the following definition of *church* from *Easton's Illustrated Dictionary of Biblical Terms:*

> Derived probably from the Greek kuriakon (i.e., the Lord's house, which was used by ancient authors for the place of worship).
>
> In the New Testament it is the translation of the Greek word ecclesia, which is synonymous with the Hebrew kahal of the Old Testament, both words meaning simply an assembly, the character of which can only be known from the connection in which the word is found. There is no clear instance of its being used for a place of meeting or of worship, although in post-apostolic times it early received this meaning. Nor is this word ever used to denote the inhabitants of a country united in the same profession, as when we say the "Church of England," the "Church of Scotland," etc. (Easton 1983)

The church clearly was designed by God to be a group of like-minded and like-believing people who live in community.

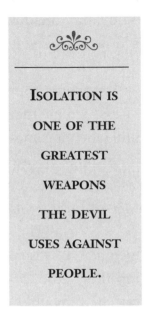

ISOLATION IS ONE OF THE GREATEST WEAPONS THE DEVIL USES AGAINST PEOPLE.

Where Two or More Are Gathered Together

The congregation that I am privileged to lead began as a small group. We have continued over the years to have small-group meetings and home fellowships. It is in small groups that people get to know others and to learn that they are facing many similar challenges and struggles.

Isolation is one of the greatest weapons the devil uses against people. Individuals can be in the middle of a crowded room and still feel isolated and alone. Small groups are conducive to spiritual growth. They provide an opportunity for people to share with one another and to "bear one another's burdens, and so fulfill the law of Christ" (Gal. 6:2 NKJV).

It is no wonder that Jesus left us with such a wonderful promise as this:

> *"Again, I tell you that if two of you on earth agree about anything you ask for, it will done for you by my Father in heaven. For where two or three come together in my name, there am I with them" (Matt. 18:19–20).*

This is reminiscent of the Bible dictionary definition of *church*. Church is not a place; it is people. Jesus makes it clear that two people qualify for *ecclesia (i.e., church)*. Now let's use this information to identify some lessons we need to learn in order for our churches to grow in prayer.

First, two people make a quorum, and those two people in agreement can pray and ask God for anything, and it will be done. God does answer our prayers, but not always the way we expect them to be answered. Usually, we have a time limit on our prayers and an expectation threshold of exactly how our prayers should be answered.

Did you know that in the King James Bible the words "but God" appear about fifty times? Those two words signify to me that God often does the unexpected. I keep that in mind when it comes to prayer, because I have expectations and time limits in my prayers too. Then I remember "but God." He has another way of doing things, and we need to be flexible in order to receive his prayer answers.

Second, when two or three people "come together" in Jesus' name (the *King James Version* says "are gathered together"), they do indeed bring him into their midst. The term "gathered together" includes in its meaning the concept of assembling. The word *midst* suggests being with, among , or in the middle of. So church could be made up of two thousand people or two people who have come or gathered together. A small group of two or more has the power to agree together and invoke God's blessings. As they do so, Jesus appears among his people, and church begins!

In no way do I believe that two or more people are required for prayers to be effective, because I am a strong believer in *individual* prayer. The point is, however, that the church needs to grow in prayer. Often we think of church only as a Sunday morning worship service or a Wednesday night prayer meeting, but it isn't. Pastors and other spiritual leaders need to unleash God's church by training them to pray as individuals, in groups of two or more, or in large congregational meetings.

The Holy Spirit's Seating Chart

In chapter five, I described how God allowed our church to purchase an old theater to use as our sanctuary. This building had three seating sections, which meant it had one aisle down each wall and two aisles down the middle. There were about 120 feet from the stage to the last row, so people in the back were a long way away. That large auditorium offered lots of room for growth.

One night, I clearly felt the Holy Spirit prompting me to do something new. God had a plan for our church, and he gave it to me step by step.

The first step was announcing that our prayer meeting would start at 5:00 P.M. sharp. People would not be allowed into the auditorium after five o'clock. You must understand that our church was comprised largely of laid-back, informal people accustomed to the flexible rules and loose timetables of a beach community. So at first it was tough on some of them who would show up five or ten minutes late. But after three or four weeks, our church members began to acquire the discipline of being on time. The Bible study and worship time started at exactly 6:00 P.M.

Step two was realizing that the Holy Spirit wanted us to grow in faith. He challenged us to believe that God would bring souls into his kingdom. At the Spirit's leading, I asked everyone to sit on the right side of the auditorium. He had promised that once we filled that entire side—front row to back row with no empty seats—he would then fill the large center section. People didn't like that! Some only wanted to arrive early in order to get a seat; others really didn't want to pray, they just wanted to sit alone on the side or in the back and not be involved. So that began a new discipline. All of this happened at the end of the hippie era, and I was dealing with undisciplined young people who did not really care for authority. But after a month, the right side filled, and we began to see the center section fill. Once the center filled, the left section began to fill. We quickly grew from a small group to a gathering of nine hundred people who came on a regular basis to seek God.

Do not ask me how or why this rapid growth happened; it just did. I heard the Lord and obeyed, and he did what he wanted to do. I think part of God's plan was to arrange things so that people would get to the services early to pray. And he was maturing our young people and teaching them to be responsible.

All of that occurred more than twenty-five years ago, and I now hand out high school diplomas to young teenagers whose mothers and fathers were in those prayer meetings and Bible studies "way back when." As I get older, I now notice that I am performing weddings for young people whose parents attended the church in those early days of revival.

Small Groups in Services

I would like to mention some specific ways that our church helps people develop the discipline of prayer, which you may want to incorporate at your own church.

One thing we do is to create small groups as part of a larger church service. On Sunday mornings, our church has a time constraint. We need to leave space between the services for people to fellowship, pick up their kids from Sunday school, and leave so that the next group can have their parking spaces. But on Saturday evenings, we have only one service and, therefore, there is no pressure to empty the building at a certain time.

After the Saturday night Bible study, I ask people to join together in groups of three to six and pray for one another. This allows shy people to listen to others praying for them, and for prayer warriors to subtly train the beginners. One of the best things about this arrangement is that it develops unity in the congregation. When individuals know that two to five people are praying a blessing on them, it has quite an impact on their lives.

Week of Fasting and Prayer

In recent years, our church has held a week of fasting and prayer a couple of times per year. Our ministerial staff members, along with the congregation, are encouraged to fast for as long as they can during that week of prayer.

Each evening during this week, we have a prayer meeting that begins at 7:00 P.M. and ends at 9:00 P.M.. People are encouraged to stay the entire two hours, but they can leave at any time. We sing two or three worship songs, I read Scripture, and then we pray. The service begins with the chairs facing the stage, and then I break the assembly into groups of five or six who circle their chairs throughout the building and begin praying together.

Each night has a different focus of music, worship, and prayer. That is, we organize the week in concentric circles of prayer. We may begin Monday evening praying for the world—crises, events, religious persecution, and needs around the planet. We pray for our missionaries and outreaches in foreign countries.

Tuesday evening we move from world prayer to national prayer. Wednesday evening we focus on state prayer, as we pray for California and its issues. Thursday evenings we pray for the city and county of San Diego. We pray for the government, fire and police and paramedics, hospitals, schools, county supervisors, the poor, kids in trouble, and anything else relating to our community. We start at one end of our county and move to the other end.

Each night we offer Communion which people can take alone or as groups. There are usually about 3,500 people praying during the week in the church, and others in their homes and via the Internet. These times allow us to grow in prayer as a church. We grow in our home fellowships and in our church services along with the groups of twos and threes who are gathered together praying daily throughout the county.

The Agape Box and Prayer Captains

For many years, we have had an "Agape Box" (or love box) in the church foyer. People who come late to the service or who miss the offering can put their coins, bills, or checks in the box on their way out. In the gymnasium, we have four similar boxes. In these boxes, we find prayer requests and financial gifts to support the maintenance of our campus. Here is what I have learned over the years: The more places people find to bring prayer to the house of God, the more prayers the church has to lift up.

Since we have a Web site, prayer requests come to us from all over the world. Since we have a national radio broadcast, prayers come to us by the dozens. And since we have places in our building where people can place their prayer requests, they come to us

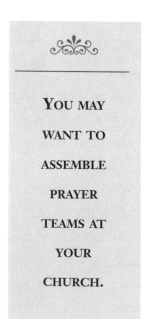

YOU MAY WANT TO ASSEMBLE PRAYER TEAMS AT YOUR CHURCH.

in great numbers and diversity of nature. Some are written on the Sunday bulletin, others on scratch pads; some are tear-stained, and some are written with crayon. These requests are distributed to people throughout our church.

Here is how we make sure that every request is prayed for: My mother, who attends our church, established a dedicated prayer team and appointed "prayer captains." As the requests pour in from around the United States and all over the world, they are given to the individual captains, who each oversee a network of men and women committed to prayer. Therefore, the captains are responsible for a certain number of requests each week, and they make sure every one of them is given individual prayer attention.

You may want to assemble prayer teams at your church. These team members need to be focused on prayer. They can never divulge the intimacy of people's lives; they must be very discreet. Let these people fall in love with prayer, and a fire of renewal and revival will break out for everyone involved.

1-800-Hit-Home

One last suggestion concerns a very effective ministry that God is using to reach youth in America. It involves two hours a week of talking with youngsters on the telephone. There is nothing like leading a troubled child or teenager to Jesus.

Here is how this ministry evolved: In 1949, Los Angeles was rocked by an earthquake. No, not the slipping of the San Andreas Fault; this was a *spiritual* earthquake. Young evangelist Billy Graham had been preaching for several weeks in what is now known as the famous Tent Crusade. It was during that time that Mr. Graham was elevated to national status in the United States. The story goes that wealthy publisher William Randolph Hearst had heard Billy preach and was blessed by the transformed lives of celebrities who were attending these Los Angeles meetings—so impressed that he put the word out to his syndication of newspapers nationwide: "Puff Graham." The rest is history.

Alice Vaus was a beautiful young Christian who had married a one-in-a-million man. Alice attended Hollywood Presbyterian Church and wanted her husband, James Arthur Vaus, to attend the Billy Graham tent meetings with her. Reluctantly, Jim went one evening, heard the Gospel of Jesus Christ, and realized that he had never surrendered his heart to God. That night Jim walked down the aisle and joined a small multitude of other Southern Californians to be born again.

I say Jim was "one-in-a-million" because he was something of a nefarious character. Jim worked with a known gangster named

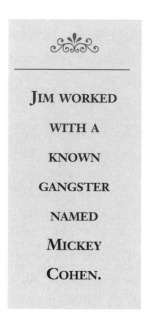

JIM WORKED WITH A KNOWN GANGSTER NAMED MICKEY COHEN.

Mickey Cohen. In 1949, Mickey Cohen had attained celebrity status. Jim was an electronics genius and was a clever and mischievous entrepreneur. I would not classify Jim as an evil man or a bad man. He was just a cunning fellow skirting on the edge of the law to make good money.

Jim had become known as the "Wire Tapper." He would tap phones so Cohen could spy on his enemies. Famous movie stars and starlets would hire Jim to tap the phones of their lovers or spouses. The Los Angeles police even used Jim to help them with some of their cases. Within a couple of years, *The Wire Tapper,* a first-run movie based on his experiences was released in theaters *nationwide.*

When Jim became a Christian, Alice was very happy, to say the least. But Jim's boss was not. Jim had crossed some members of the mob, and they were angry. (If you have ever seen the movie *The Sting* featuring Paul Newman and Robert Redford, you can understand Jim's dilemma.)

Jim knew where the bookie joints were, and he knew how to delay the broadcast from the racetracks to these joints where bets were being placed on them. Before he became a Christian, he would set up his scam and delay the race broadcast by a minute or so; then, knowing the results, he would send his partner in to bet on the race before he released the broadcast. After winning so

MICKEY SPENT SEVERAL MEETINGS ALONE WITH JIM, CLIFF BARROWS, AND BILLY GRAHAM.

many races, Mickey and "the boys" became suspicious of Jim's big winnings and their big losses. Ultimately, Jim's partner was killed over this scam. Mickey and some of his hard-hitting thugs threatened Jim, who just responded that he was born again and that all his past was gone and forgiven.

Supernaturally, God intervened in Jim's life and spared him. Mickey spent several meetings alone with Jim, Cliff Barrows, and Billy Graham. Though Cohen tried his best to become a believer, some question whether he ever actually did so.

Since Jim loved working with kids, he began a work in New York City in one of the roughest neighborhoods of Harlem called Hell's Gate. Jim, with a lot of prayer and very little money, opened a storefront as a place of refuge for troubled kids. He held Bible studies and other activities to keep the kids away from the gangs and off the streets after school. He eventually purchased property outside the city with the help of George Champion, chairman of the board of Chase Manhattan Bank. Jim's camps turned around hundreds of lost and wayward children. Many today are corporate executives. I know of a woman influenced by Jim's work who later earned a Ph.D. and is now a professor at San Diego State University.

Jim moved to San Diego with his family and continued his ministry, called Youth Development Incorporated. When I met Jim, he turned over his ministry to me to continue the work. That included a hotline, today known as 1-800-Hit-Home.

About 10,000 kids call every month seeking help and guidance. Many of these kids just want someone to talk with. Our son

Phillip now heads that ministry and has a heart for these youngsters. They aren't all runaways or juvenile delinquents; in fact, many of them are kids from Christian homes. On our campus there is a computer that is dedicated to 1-800-Hit-Home. The calls come in from all fifty states and are routed to churches and individual Christians all around the country. These people talk and pray with the children and teens on the line. When a phone number is busy, the computer automatically transfers the call to the next person who is assigned to that time slot.

Unfortunately, 35 percent of all phone calls go unanswered because of a lack of counselors and prayer warriors. Maybe this is a way that your church could grow in prayer. Join with our church, and we can multiply the number of youth in America who have the opportunity to hear about Jesus.

> NEVER BEFORE HAS THE WORLD NEEDED PRAYER WARRIORS AS MUCH IT NEEDS THEM TODAY.

Unleash the Power

The Bible tells us that when the church first began gathering together, it was for prayer. On the Day of Pentecost, 120 believers gathered together in a room, and as they prayed the Holy Ghost fell upon them. Their spirits were so ignited that they began to speak with other tongues and to prophesy.

Later, as the new body of believers began to multiply, we see throughout the book of Acts that Christians believed mightily in prayer and the power that was associated with prayer:

And when they had prayed, the place where they were assembled together was shaken; and they were all filled with the Holy Spirit, and they spoke the word of God with boldness (Acts 4:31 NKJV).

Never before has the world needed prayer warriors as much it needs them today. The church has never needed the power to pray as much as it does today. As we fall in love with prayer, we will see God's Spirit unleashed in our individual lives, our churches, and our communities.

CHAPTER EIGHT

GROWING IN PRAYER

"The more you pray, the easier it becomes.
The easier it becomes, the more you will pray."
MOTHER TERESA

When I was a teenager I wanted so much to be accepted by my peers, and I decided that a foul mouth was a way to act like a man. I noticed that most men swore and told dirty stories. So by the time I was twenty years old, I had developed an extensive vocabulary of swear words. There were not many filthy stories I didn't know either, and those I knew I repeated as often as possible. If there had been an Environmental Protection Agency in those days, I am sure my mouth would have been quarantined for the safety of society.

In the spring of 1970, I had just accepted Jesus as my Lord and Savior. Right from the start, I knew that daily prayer and Bible reading were imperative for me. One morning as I was praying and having my devotions, I suddenly felt as if a lightning bolt had hit me in the center of my mind. I realized that I had gone seven days without saying a swear word or telling a dirty story or thinking of anything filthy. It had only been one week since I dedicated myself to Jesus, but my prayers and the purifying work of the

I HAD ALWAYS HAD A MEAN STREAK IN ME THAT DROVE ME TO "GET EVEN" WITH PEOPLE.

Holy Spirit had already made dramatic changes in my life. From that day until this one, the blood of Jesus Christ has cleansed my mind and mouth.

Here is another way that God worked in my life: I had always had a mean streak in me that drove me to try to "get even" with people. Pent-up anger from my childhood followed me into adulthood. Then one day I found myself in a situation that some years earlier would have ended in a verbal barrage of devastating consequences. But this time I felt no need to lash out. It dawned on me that Jesus had taken from me this deep-seated anger.

When I think about the changes that have occurred in me, I recall this passage:

> *The acts of the sinful nature are obvious: sexual immorality, impurity and debauchery; idolatry and witchcraft; hatred, discord, jealousy, fits of rage, selfish ambition, dissensions, factions and envy; drunkenness, orgies, and the like. I warn you, as I did before, that those who live like this will not inherit the kingdom of God (Gal. 5:19–21).*

Now when I read this text, I can see that these works of the flesh have been removed from me ever so gently. By nature, I was the complete picture of this outline by the apostle Paul. I was self-centered, ambitious, envious, and a drunkard. I was filled with anger, wrath, hatred, and jealousy. Was there any hope that I could ever overcome such toxic and self-destructive tendencies? Yes, there was: it was through Jesus Christ.

All of these things that Jesus took from me he began replacing with the wonderful qualities Paul mentions in the following verses:

> *But the fruit of the Spirit is love, joy, peace, patience,*
> *kindness, goodness, faithfulness, gentleness and self-control.*
> *Against such there is no law (Gal. 5:22–23).*

Like you, I find it so refreshing to know that I am growing in the Lord. Gentleness replaced anger and wrath. Joy and peace dispelled the party spirit. Self-control took away the drunkenness and drugs.

Just as we can look at our past failures and wrongs and see them in the light of God's love and grace in our spiritual lives, so we must see growth in our prayer lives. We must grow beyond rote and repetitive prayers such as "Now I lay me down to sleep" and "Bless this food." Our prayer life should become ever richer, fuller, and more joyful as we learn to talk with our heavenly Father.

You don't need a prayer monitor to watch over your growth. Just take my challenge and listen to your own prayers, and you will see that you are growing in prayer. The more your prayers turn from self to others, the more you can count on spiritual growth. As God removes issue after issue from your life, you will see that you are *praising* God more than *begging* God. You will grow in prayer, and as you do, your spirit will grow along with your relationship with God.

My point is this: One of the best ways to develop your prayer life is to be attentive to the changes and growth that are occurring in your life as a result of prayer. The more you grow, the more you will want to pray.

With these thoughts in mind, let me mention some practical ways to grow in the area of prayer:

Reflex Prayer

Early in my Christian life, I learned about something I have come to call "reflex prayer." Most of us have been in a doctor's office sitting up with our legs dangling over the end of the exam table. The physician tells us to relax and begins tapping lightly below our kneecap. When the little hammer hits just the right the spot, our leg jerks up in the air. He is, of course, testing our reflexes to see that our muscular and nervous systems are working properly. Well, that is a good picture of what I mean by the term reflex prayer.

Has someone ever said to you, "Please pray for me"? and you say, "Sure, I'd be glad to." Then you walk away and forget all about it. After a couple of days, it hits you that this friend asked for prayer, but you cannot remember what in the world you were supposed to pray about. At that point, the devil loves to begin condemning you, and the guilt gets piled on like pastrami in a New York deli. That used to happen to me a lot until I came to understand the verse that says, "Pray without ceasing" (1 Thess. 5:17 NKJV). Reflex prayer releases you from the load of guilt for prayers you promised to say but never delivered.

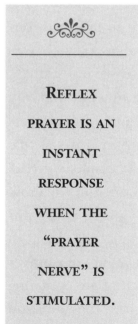

REFLEX PRAYER IS AN INSTANT RESPONSE WHEN THE "PRAYER NERVE" IS STIMULATED.

Reflex prayer is not necessarily a knee-jerk reaction; rather, it is an instant response when the "prayer nerve" is stimulated. I learned this fact from my pastor,

Chuck Smith, who had graciously let me teach a Wednesday night Bible study when I was only two years old in the Lord. Because hundreds of people attended, a line would inevitably form after a service was finished. Folks would want to discuss the lesson or share prayer requests.

Many people would say to me, "Mike, will you pray for me?"

I wouldn't just respond, "Sure, I'll pray for you." Instead, I would say, "Yes. In fact, let's pray right now." And we would take a few seconds or a few minutes to pray then and there.

That way my "obligation" was fulfilled, and I would not have to write anything down or try to remember any details. Nor would I have any guilt if I forgot to pray altogether.

I recall a man named Keith Ritter, who was the special assistant to the owner of a beer company. Keith was a successful businessman who owned a realty company in Newport Beach, California. Keith left business to serve the Lord, and he was on the board of directors of Calvary Chapel when it first started its phenomenal growth explosion in the early seventies. Keith was a teaching elder and assisted the pastor, Chuck Smith, when needed.

After a few years, Keith felt called to serve in Asia, so he and his wife, Sue, moved to Hong Kong to help spread the Gospel to the Chinese. Some time later, Keith came back to California and had an appointment with Chuck to discuss the work in Hong Kong.

A week after that meeting, I saw Chuck and noticed that he was wearing a new watch. Having been to Hong Kong myself, I realized that this kind of watch was not available in the States. It had one of the first microchips in it that allowed the time to show in digital numbers. And by pushing a button on the side, you could follow an arrow on the face that displayed time zones all over the planet. When you wanted to know what time it was anywhere in the world, you just pressed the button. That may seem passé by today's technological standards, but in 1973 it was quite a novelty.

When I noticed the watch, I said, "That's a cool watch, Chuck. I saw one just like it when I was in Hong Kong."

Chuck told me about his meeting with Keith Ritter, and how he had been fascinated with Keith's watch. Keith took it off and said, "Here, Chuck, take it. It's a gift from me. All I ask is that when you look at it, you remember to pray for me."

Then Chuck told me that he wouldn't take it for free and instead gave Keith a hundred dollars for it. Why? So he wouldn't feel the responsibility to pray for Keith, in case he forgot. The watch would not be a constant guilt-inducing reminder that Chuck had failed in his prayer obligation.

Now that may seem silly, but it was said in a fun-loving manner. Chuck was making the point that he would pray for Keith, but by paying for the watch he wouldn't be praying out of a sense of obligation to keep a rigid rule. That is another example of reflex prayer: Look at the watch, pray for Keith.

Reflex prayer for me is simpler than having buzzwords or icons to remind me to pray. Some people do, in fact, set an alarm clock to remind them to pray, or keep a running prayer list in their calendar. If that kind of thing works for you, then that's terrific. As for me, I prefer to pray on the spot and at the moment so the request doesn't disappear among all the details and minutiae overflowing in my brain.

This type of praying makes it easy to fall in love with prayer. On Sunday mornings at church, I usually speak with dozens of people before, after, and in between services. I have found that my time is used more effectively by praying with people on the spot than it would be if I made appointments for all those people to come and see me during the week.

Many times I have found that what might take up an entire one-hour appointment can be taken care of with a handshake, a few minutes of listening, and a simple statement, "Let's pray." The reflex is to handle the situation right then, not days later.

This has become such a part of me that I am not at all inhibited to pray with a complete stranger—anywhere, anytime the need arises. So my encouragement to you is, meet that prayer need right then and there.

Get Inspired by Prayer Classics

I enjoy reading books by and about ministers of the 1800s and early 1900s. During that period there existed an era of spiritual awakening in Great Britain and the United States that had deep roots in prayer.

Many wonderful pastors and Bible teachers grew up during that era and blessed the body of Christ worldwide. A large number of men and women responded to the move of the Holy Spirit and entered the mission field. David Livingstone went to Africa; Hudson Taylor went to China; D. L. Moody went with one arm wrapped around America and the other around England and Scotland. Wonderful pastor-teachers such as Charles Spurgeon, F. B. Meyer, G. Campbell Morgan, and D. Martin Lloyd-Jones all were tremendous in-depth Bible teachers with hearts of prayer. Let me point out just a few of my most admired Christian forebears.

D. L. Moody

Dwight L. Moody is one of my "heroes of the faith" because of his simple nature. There is a common thread running through all the books I have read about him and his life and ministry: Moody was a man deeply committed to prayer and seeking God's face.

This gregarious evangelist was instrumental in the Sunday school movement throughout the United States. He loved children and ministered to them while he was in Chicago. It was nothing for Moody's Sunday school class to have a couple of hundred children in it. Moody was one of the earliest proponents and supporters of the YMCA, the Young Men's Christian Association (though I think today he would be surprised to learn what has become of it).

Recently, I republished the only biography of D. L. Moody that he ever authorized and endorsed. (Mann and Moody 1997) It was written by his son, and it is a story that not only captivates but also motivates the reader. Moody did not want to be glorified nor have any attention placed upon him that should be given to Jesus Christ. He established orphanages, churches, Bible schools, and children's ministries, and preached to tens of thousands of people at a time. This man led people into the kingdom of God in Ireland, Scotland, Wales, England, and throughout the United States. In fact, he held an evangelistic crusade in San Diego in 1891. I imagine some of those seeds he planted there have come to fruition in my lifetime, and I have had the privilege of harvesting that fruit more than a century later.

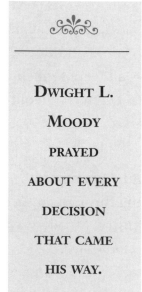

DWIGHT L. MOODY PRAYED ABOUT EVERY DECISION THAT CAME HIS WAY.

You will enjoy reading the sermons and stories of encounters Moody had with atheists and nonbelievers. Like Jesus, he was so down to earth that "the common people heard him gladly" (Mark 12:37 KJV). Before his conversion experience, he was a shoe salesman in Chicago. He was a very good salesman, in fact, and many business leaders later gave money to the godly causes Moody started or supported.

His gift of gab was used by the Holy Spirit to make him a great speaker. Indeed, he was a persuasive communicator even though his detractors freely criticized his poor grasp of the English language. His education was slim, and therefore his poor grammar put off listeners, especially the elitists in the crowds.

Dwight L. Moody prayed about every decision that came his way. He prayed for the people he was about to preach to. He prayed for the thousands and thousands of dollars that were necessary to start up the myriad endeavors he undertook for God's kingdom. He was a delightful man to be around, we are told—a jovial man with a quick wit and a refreshing sense of humor. He had a tender heart for God, and it was reflected in his care and concern for lost sinners.

That type of heart comes from hours of prayer. It comes from waiting on the answers to prayer and from receiving the answers to prayer. It seems obvious that the more we sit at the feet of the Lord in prayer, the more of his attributes we take on.

Andrew Murray

This is another man who has influenced my life in the area of devotion and prayer. Though I could recommend several titles that would be inspiring and informative, his classic work *With Christ in the School of Prayer* is a must. He wrote this book in South Africa in the nineteenth century. Murray was a Spirit-filled Dutch Reformed pastor who has influenced more people toward prayer in the past hundred years than probably any other gifted writer or minister.

Murray once said: "The place and power of prayer in the Christian life is too little understood." I couldn't agree more.

Andrew Murray influenced D. L. Moody, and I think it was a two-way street. I heard that R. A. Torrey, who was a contemporary of Moody's, would share the platform with Andrew Murray and D. L. Moody at evangelistic outreaches. Torrey had a tremendous message concerning the baptism of the Holy Spirit and the Christian life of walking in the Spirit, while Moody's message was the love and saving grace of Jesus Christ, and Murray's emphasis was a Christian walk in faith, devotion, and prayer. Imagine being in a meeting with those three dynamos preaching!

George Mueller

One of the biographies about this man that has encouraged me is *George Muller, Man of Faith and Miracles.* (Miller 1941) He was from England, and his ministry inspired many of his contemporaries to be people of faith and prayer.

Recently a friend sent me a Website link that showed photos of the orphanages Mueller built by faith. Whenever I think about this man, I recall a story that has stayed with me throughout the years: One morning, the boys in one of his orphanages were getting ready for breakfast, and the headmaster told Mueller that there was no food in the house. Mueller responded by saying, "Have you prayed?" Yes, of course, they had prayed.

With that settled, Mueller assured the headmaster that everything would be all right. A few minutes later, there was a knock at the kitchen door. The milkman had broken an axle on his wagon, and the goods would spoil by the time he could get it fixed. Could the orphanage use the milk and eggs and cheese? Soon another knock came, and this time it was the baker. He had an overrun on rolls and breads. Could the orphanage use the extra food?

One month some bills were due, and the orphanage came up two pennies short. George wasn't satisfied because God always provided *everything* for his work. So the workers prayed and prayed. Then they went to the alms box, and inside were two pennies.

Mueller is a fascinating study in faith and in prayer. I commend him, along with Moody and Murray, to your reading. Lives like theirs have brought forth so much fruit, and they are examples of the fruit God will bring through you and me once we fall in love with prayer.

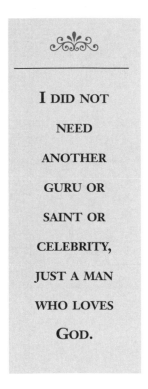

I DID NOT NEED ANOTHER GURU OR SAINT OR CELEBRITY, JUST A MAN WHO LOVES GOD.

An Example to Follow

I fell in love with prayer simply because my pastor, Chuck Smith, became my role model. He loves to pray. I am not sure there is a more spiritually rounded minister than the pastor to whom God led me. His devotion to God is crowned with a prayer life full of love.

As a very young Christian, I prayed for some specific things. Having been deceived through mysticism, the occult, and Eastern religions, I asked God, "Give me a man who simply loves you and loves the Bible—a man who will teach me the Bible and not try to make me his disciple." I didn't say "and a man who loves prayer," because I didn't know about the power of prayer. But I got that man, and does he love to pray. I did not need another guru or saint or celebrity, just a man who loves God.

As I look back upon the progress that I have made in my spiritual life, I sense within me a strong desire to grow more and more in the discipline of prayer. I want to become a man of faith and prayer for many more of God's children as I grow older and increase in spiritual maturity. I pray that I will be successful in my efforts to raise up in my own church and community people who understand the incredible power of prayer. And I pray that you too will come to understand and appreciate that incredible power so that you can be ever more effective in your own prayers and in spreading the love of prayer to all those in your sphere of influence.

CHAPTER NINE

PRAYING WITH THE RIGHT ATTITUDE

*"The purpose of all prayer is to find God's will
and to make that will our prayer."*
CATHERINE MARSHALL

According to the CIA, Romania is considered one of the poorest countries of Central and Eastern Europe. In 1989, the totalitarian regime that ran the country was overthrown. The government control had left the beautiful people of that country in poverty. They were saddled with an obsolete industrial base and a business climate that basically was only for the elite.

Nicolae Ceausescu, the despotic leader of that nation for many years, was the son of a peasant. His rule was extremely repressive and corrupt, according to reports from inside and outside the country. He lived from 1918 until 1989, when an uprising involving the populace and the military took place. As a result, Nicolae and wife, Elena, were arrested and executed.

I had the privilege of traveling to Romania twice: once in 1977 and again in 1987. Both times it was obvious to me that there was a dictator in power. The basic necessities of life were rationed in the big cities, villages, and countryside. Secret police were everywhere, spying on the Romanian people and, of course, on Americans like me who were visiting their country.

My purpose for being there was not political but spiritual. I was in Romania to share the Gospel of Jesus Christ. It was extremely difficult for the people to host a guest because of the lack of food. Because of this situation, as we traveled to various churches, God was able to plant some deep truths into my heart and soul—lessons that I cherish to this day.

Christians Under Persecution

The first lesson came in 1977 in the lovely town of Oradea. The city is about ten kilometers from Hungary in the northwest portion of Romania and today has a population of approximately 225,000 people.

I had just finished speaking for three weeks in Poland, Czechoslovakia, and Hungary, and was invited to teach in Romanian churches. An elder in the church met me and my companions at a prearranged site in downtown Oradea, with its beautiful buildings and architecture representing centuries of design. There were three of us, and we went to dinner at the home of this church leader.

He was dressed very humbly, wearing an old, tattered suit jacket and probably the only pair of "dress" pants he owned. His home was on a street in need of repair and, as it was for all those struggling to make ends meet, his house was run-down. Seven beautiful children were in this family, and his wife greeted us with tremendous warmth and joy. To have an American Bible teacher come in those days was apparently a real treat. I was humbled to enter this home so obviously filled with Christian love.

I noticed the modest setting in which this large family lived together. There was one large living room, a kitchen, and a master bedroom with a bathroom. Nothing more. It had a small courtyard that separated the street and sidewalk from the front door of the house so there was a gate that provided some privacy. Remember, under communist rule, Christianity was not always tolerated, and there was a price to pay for one's faith. I thought often of Jesus' words:

> *"Blessed are those who are persecuted because of right-eousness, for theirs is the kingdom of heaven.*
> *"Blessed are you when people insult you, persecute you and falsely say all kinds of evil against you because of me. Rejoice and be glad, because great is your reward in heaven, for in the same way they persecuted the prophets who were before you"* (Matt. 5:10–12).

Christians in Poverty

WE BOWED OUR HEADS, AND THE FATHER OF THIS GODLY HOUSEHOLD PRAYED.

When we sat down to eat, this family positioned me at the head of the table. It was a very kind gesture, to say the least. The children stood around the table, and I asked them to join us. The warmth of their smiles was so contagious that it made me feel as though I was surrounded by angels.

We bowed our heads, and the father of this godly household prayed. The softness and gentleness of his prayer caught my attention. Then the gratefulness and thanksgiving toward God became more and more evident. The focus of this man on his Creator was amazing to behold. Then as he asked a blessing on our journey and the evening's event, he closed as if he were standing before God himself: "In the name of Jesus Christ our Lord and Savior, amen."

The dinner was set before us, and the children, still standing, smiled and nodded for us to please eat. My nature would have been to try to convince them to eat with us, but then I saw the meal. Each of us had one slice of bread with butter on it and a slice of green pepper. The main course was soup made of hot water and half of a peeled baked potato. Then it hit me as if I were walking down a street and a piano had fallen on top of me: This was all the food this family had, and they were giving it to total strangers in the name of their Lord.

When I was finished, I asked if I could use the bathroom, and they pointed the way through an open door adjoining the bedroom. I closed the door behind me and walked through their bedroom. I noticed on the way that there were little ceramic animals on the dresser. Nothing fancy, nothing expensive. If you were to buy them in the United States at a discount store, they would probably cost a dollar or two each.

That evening 1,500 people gathered in a non–air-conditioned church auditorium, and they sang as if there was no tomorrow. A Romanian from Paris, France, aged eighty sat down and played "How Great Thou Art" on a saw. That's right—a saw. Before I taught from the book of Revelation, I was completely at peace with God and thoroughly humbled in the presence of so many believers who were sacrificing greatly to worship God publicly in an atheistic country.

Later, as we went to our car downtown, our host handed me a small brown paper sack. I thanked him from my heart for all of his kindness and prayed with him. Then we parted ways.

Opening my little paper bag, I reached inside and brought out the gift from my Romanian brother. It was one of the ceramic dogs that had been on his nightstand: a gray and white wire-haired terrier that had an obvious crack in it and had been glued together.

It certainly was not necessary for him to give me anything. I never charge for speaking engagements and often return any honorarium offered to me. Yet in his poverty, this man gave me something that was truly a treasure to him. It is a wonderful gift that I cherish to this day.

What a contrast between the humble, self-giving attitude that motivated this sacrificial act of love and gratitude in the midst of an oppressive atheistic society, and the arrogant, self-serving attitude of many believers in the affluent and acquisitive "Christian" societies of the world.

Materialistic Churches

In today's Western civilization, materialism has reached an all-time high. Obtaining material possessions is the goal of this present age of consumerism. Unfortunately, this attitude is also found in the churches of Western society.

A year ago, I was reading some information about churches in the United States. I do not remember the exact numbers, but these are close, and you will get my gist. Of more than 400,000 churches in America, the average church has between seventy-five and one hundred members. The average annual budget is about $100,000 per year. The average giving is 1 to 3 percent of the annual income of those who give. And the point that got my attention is that there is around $1 billion in building loans to churches.

I found that information to be incredible because it means that the church as a whole is essentially bankrupt. For small churches, financial debt is a problem that hinders them from growing and expanding. For large churches, debt is a problem because now the church creates programs to draw people to the ministry—ulti-mately, the reason for ministry is "more people, more money." This is a vicious cycle because to pay off the debt is almost impos-sible for some, and yet the desire to minister tugs at the heart of church staff members all over America. Some pastoral staffs believe that "bigger is better," and with that mindset comes striv-ing to meet debt and to restructure loans. The church is trapped because of worldly concepts and worldly methods.

One man in the United States has a ministry to help people with their finances—budgeting, reducing debt, and so on. He has written several best-selling books and is a well-respected speaker at major conferences. I respect him, but I won't support him. Let me tell you why.

One day as I was opening my mail, I came across a monthly mailer from this man's ministry. Every evangelical ministry is easy to spot on the first and the fifteenth of the month by their "appeal letters" written as if we were personal, long-time friends. Each one explains how important it is that we respond to the immediate need. Included is a return envelope with a card that shows Visa, Discover, MasterCard, and American Express logos at the bottom. There are also boxes to check to indicate a donation of $25, $50, $100, $500, $1000, or "Other." Then there is usually a line to be signed that reads, "I promise by faith to give monthly as God provides."

Well, when I received a form letter from the financial guidance counselor

I WADDED UP THE COMPUTER-PRINTED LETTER AND SLAM-DUNKED IT INTO THE NEAREST GARBAGE CAN.

whose books I had read and whose approach I had liked, I came to the main point: The letter said that this organization was in debt and was in need of $2 to $3 million dollars immediately. With the economy in recession and high unemployment, this man's ministry was in trouble.

I wadded up the computer-printed letter and slam-dunked it into the nearest garbage can. How could someone who is telling us to trust his debt-relief principles find himself millions of dollars in debt? If his "biblical" principles are not working for him, then why should we follow his advice? Isn't that a case of "the blind leading the blind"?

I am not trying to sound cynical, and I don't mean to ridicule anyone in particular. The point is that thousands of Americans donate millions of dollars to organizations and spend millions on conferences, videos, cassette tapes, DVDs, and books in the "how-to market" of Christianity. They spend hours and hours studying these products and attending pep rally seminars—yet many of them won't invest one hour in personal quiet prayer time.

What people spend their time, money, and energy on indicates what is most important to them; it reveals their core values. This applies to the church as much as it does to the world.

Distorted Values

It would be a vast understatement to say that there is a problem in the church today. The truth is that churches need to grow in prayer just as individuals need to grow in prayer, as I have mentioned in previous chapters. When individuals grow in their own prayer life, they begin to see that not everything that glitters is gold.

Sergeant Bob has been with the San Diego Police Department longer than I have, and I have been there twenty-two years. He is a decorated Vietnam veteran, a husband, and a father. When I

131

first met him with a mutual police officer friend, we walked into Bob's office and shook hands. I noticed the memorabilia on the desk and shelves, and then I saw something I had never seen before. On his wall was an irregular-shaped object the size of a Frisbee®, obviously spray-painted a metallic gold. Underneath this unique piece of art were the words, "Everything that glitters is not gold!"

The sergeant saw me looking at it and asked, "Do you know what that is?"

"No," I replied. "I've never seen anything like it."

He told me that he is from Oklahoma, and that every year he goes back with his family to visit his parents and relatives. At the county fair, they have a "cow pie" throwing contest. He entered the previous year and won the trophy for the longest throw. This was his trophy—a "golden" cow pie. A bit crude perhaps, but it makes a good point. Sergeant Bob is a homicide detective, and this trophy and inscription always remind him that not everything is as it appears. He needs to keep looking for clues and asking questions to find the truth.

That story reminds me that we, as Christians, must be vigilant and truth seeking when it comes to our faith. We can so easily become misguided and deceived, but prayer provides the means through which the Holy Spirit can lead us and direct us.

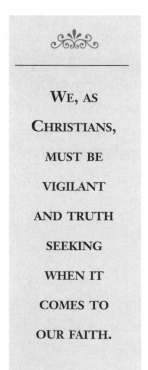

WE, AS CHRISTIANS, MUST BE VIGILANT AND TRUTH SEEKING WHEN IT COMES TO OUR FAITH.

Self-centered Doctrines

There are many shallow doctrines in the church today that ulti-

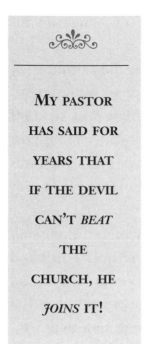

MY PASTOR
HAS SAID FOR
YEARS THAT
IF THE DEVIL
CAN'T *BEAT*
THE
CHURCH, HE
JOINS IT!

mately are nothing more than distractions sent from the enemy. These distractions often keep people from gaining spiritual fruit from their prayers. My pastor has said for years that if the devil can't *beat* the church, he *joins* it!

Some churches teach the power of "positive confession," which asserts that people's own words can make them or break them. Even though this is not a doctrine of Jesus Christ or the apostles or Moses or biblical prophets, people still follow it. Their teachers control them from the first introduction of the doctrine because it would be a negative confession to deny it or to challenge it. The issue here, for all of us, is about the *self*. What does the Gospel have for *me*? Selfishness is about control, and control is easy to come by if we can just "name it and claim it" or speak in a positive manner. Christians in any of the Third World countries in which I have traveled are unlikely to adhere to such a doctrine. In fact, they might view the propagator of it as a false prophet. Philosophies promoting the idea that God wants his children to be rich and prosperous work best in a materialistic society, because poor societies have few resources for Christians to gain wealth.

This materialistic, "God wants you rich" philosophy is definitely different from the words of our Lord. As Jesus said to his disciples, "If anyone would come after me, he must deny himself and take up his cross and follow me. For whoever wants to save his life will lose it, but whoever loses his life for me will find it. What good will it be for a man if he gains the whole world, yet forfeits his soul? Or what can a man give in exchange for his soul?" (Matt. 16:24–26).

Jesus was not impressed with materialism. He didn't clutter his ministry or his personal life with an abundance of things. Jesus told his followers: "Watch out! Be on your guard against all kinds of greed; a man's life does not consist in the abundance of his possessions'" (Luke 12:15). He also said, "Foxes have holes and birds of the air have nests, but the Son of Man has nowhere to lay His head" (Matt. 8:20 NKJV).

How is it that the church can have such a wonderful mission from heaven and such amazing power from the Holy Spirit and such a wonderful leader as Jesus Christ, and yet go astray and miss the mark again and again? I think it has to do with the shallowness of believers and their lack of commitment to prayer. The enemy knows that if he can keep a church or a believer away from prayer, he can keep them from the power and glory of heaven.

That's why it is so important not only to read and study the Scriptures but also to properly understand, interpret, and apply them in our lives—especially our prayer lives.

Twisting Scripture

You may have heard of the book *The Prayer of Jabez*, and perhaps you have even read it. It created quite a sensation for several years. The book industry publication *Publisher's Weekly* called it one of the fastest-selling books of all time.

A *New York Times* best-seller for several months, the book is based on a simple prayer found in the Old Testament. I prefer to call it the "misunderstood prayer of Jabez." I know the author of this book and remember him from when his ministry first began. I respect him and believe his intention in writing this book was sincere and honest. I also believe that many people have taken the author's point and twisted it for their own personal fulfillment. That is, many people have taken Jabez's prayer for *spiritual* blessing and prosperity and turned it into a formula for receiving *physical* blessing and prosperity.

The prayer is found in 1 Chronicles 4:10. When we study this brief biblical passage, we begin to see its true intent and purpose. Let's review it in several different translations:

New Living Translation: "He [Jabez] was the one who prayed to the God of Israel, 'Oh, that you would bless me and extend my lands! Please be with me in all that I do, and keep me from all trouble and pain!' And God granted him his request." This translation of the prayer seems to indicate that Jabez was asking for more material blessings and goods from God and personal preservation from "all trouble and pain."

Revised Standard Version: "Jabez called on the God of Israel, saying, 'Oh that thou wouldst bless me and enlarge my border, and that thy hand might be with me, and that thou wouldst keep me from harm so that it might not hurt me!' And God granted what he asked." In this translation also, Jabez seems to be asking God for more blessings and land and personal protection from harm and hurt.

American Standard Version: "And Jabez called on the God of Israel, saying, Oh that thou wouldest bless me indeed, and enlarge my border, and that thy hand might be with me, and that thou wouldest keep me from evil, that it be not to my sorrow! And God granted him that which he requested." Notice the slight change in the prayer of Jabez as interpreted in this translation. Blessings and enlargement of borders are the same. Being kept from evil is closer to the truth, and the desire that evil would not be to his sorrow is more in keeping with God's will.

New American Standard Bible (1977 version): "Now Jabez called on the God of Israel, saying, 'Oh that Thou wouldst bless me indeed, and enlarge my border, and that Thy hand might be with me, and that Thou wouldst keep me from harm, that it may not pain me!' And God granted him what he requested." Take note that in the more modern version the end of the prayer is "that it may not pain me!"

Finally, let's look at two more translations:.

King James Version: "And Jabez called on the God of Israel, saying, Oh that thou wouldest bless me indeed, and enlarge my coast, and that thine hand might be with me, and that thou wouldest keep me from evil, that it may not grieve me! And God granted him that which he requested." The blessings remain, and the gaining of more land is still there, but being kept from evil is a bit clearer as is the idea that evil not grieve Jabez.

New King James Version: "And Jabez called on the God of Israel saying, 'Oh, that You would bless me indeed, and enlarge my territory, that Your hand would be with me, and that You would keep me from evil, that I may not cause pain!' So God granted him what he requested." Again, notice that the basics are the same in this translation. The difference between this translation and the other translations is in what it shows to be the real point of the prayer— "that you [God] would keep me from evil, that I may not *cause pain*!" (emphasis added).

This translation really stands out to me because of the last sentence. Mainly, it speaks to me because of the meaning of the name *Jabez* in the Hebrew language. According to *The International Standard Bible Encyclopedia* (Orr 1988) this name *Jabez* is "interpreted as if it stood for" another Hebrew expression meaning "he causes pain." The author of this entry goes on to say, "His request was granted, 'and the sorrow implied by his ominous name was averted by prayer.'"

PEOPLE ARE OFTEN MORE INTERESTED IN PROSPERITY IN THE *PHYSICAL* REALM THAN THEY ARE IN PROSPERITY IN THE *SPIRITUAL* REALM.

Wanting the Right Things

The average person, of course, likes the idea of having more land, more prosperity, and more safety and protection. We all want those things. Yet when we examine the context of the prayer of Jabez, we see something that most people usually don't want to take responsibility for, so they pass over it.

This is one of the main problems with the practice of prayer today in the church. People are often more interested in prosperity in the *physical* realm than they are in prosperity in the *spiritual* realm.

In more than thirty years of reading and studying the Bible, I have been amazed at how the Jewish people were able to give names to their children at birth and then see those names borne out in their children's lives. In the case of Jabez, we see that his name "sounds like the Hebrew for *pain*" (see the footnote to 1 Chron. 4:9). This tells me that something probably happened at his birth. He could have been a premature baby, which would have caused pain to his mother. Or maybe he was born breech, or there could have been some other complication with the delivery, which could also have caused pain.

It all points to the fact that there was pain in his birth and that pain may have followed him his whole life. Taken in context, it seems that Jabez's prayer came at a time in his life when he was getting ready for something big, and he needed God's help. It could have been that he was preparing to go to war against the Canaanites. He may have needed God's protection and help to expand "his" borders for the sake of Israel. If so, his prayer wasn't a selfish request for his own prosperity; he wanted God to prevent him from fulfilling the name his mother had given him.

What Do You Seek?

Hopefully, you can see the fallacy of some Christian teaching these days—particularly the idea that prayer is calling upon *God* to do what he has promised—for *our* benefit as well as the benefit of others. The implication is that if we have received a "word of faith" from God and have planted our "seed faith" in his work, then *God is obligated to respond to us in accordance to his promise to bless us physically as well as spiritually.* ... This is often referred to as believing, confessing, and acting on God's Word.

Read carefully the words of Jesus Christ and let the Holy Spirit open the eyes of your understanding:

> *"Do not set your heart on what you will eat or drink; do not worry about it. For the pagan world runs after all such things, and your Father knows that you need them. But seek his kingdom, and these things will be given to you as well" (Luke 12:29–31).*

In this passage, Jesus makes it clear that there are things we *should* seek, and there are things that we *should not* seek. God is aware of our basic needs and necessities. He has promised to provide those for us. Our responsibility is to seek his kingdom—period.

When we seek his kingdom, he provides the necessary things for us while we receive the joy of seeing him work on our behalf. The problem in an affluent society is that we don't have many one- or two-dollar ceramic figurines that we cherish as much as a

JESUS MAKES IT CLEAR THAT THERE ARE THINGS WE *SHOULD* SEEK, AND THERE ARE THINGS THAT WE *SHOULD NOT* SEEK.

five-thousand-dollar Rolex watch. We can order steak and lobster any time we want; we don't have to settle for watered-down soup with a chunk of potato.

We have so much excess and abundance, yet we keep asking for more. We are a spoiled people with too much money and too much time on our hands; therefore, we really do not need to *seek* very often because all of our needs are fulfilled before we even ask ... If we do have a need, the dividend check is in the mail, or the American Express card will cover it. When the credit line is over its limit, we still have Visa and MasterCard in which to trust. We have obviously carried worldly thinking into our spiritual lives.

The bottom line is this: Prayer has little to do with possessions, money, and things. It has *everything* to do with deepening our relationship with the Lord, growing into the person he wants us to become, and seeking to expand and enrich his kingdom. We all must learn to pray with the right attitude and perspective—that God's kingdom will increase and that we may have the awesome privilege of participating in his mission to save mankind. That is at the very heart of prayer.

CHAPTER TEN

PRAYER PAYS OFF PERSONALLY

"He who ceases to pray ceases to prosper."
WILLIAM GURNEY BENHAM

Recently, I saw a newspaper editorial cartoon that illustrated the power of prayer. It showed two rows of black silhouettes. Lined up in the first row was a battleship next to an army tank next to a Predator unmanned aircraft. In the second row, there was a B-52 bomber next to a stealth fighter next to a woman kneeling down in a church pew with her head bowed and obviously praying. Her prayer was: "Release the POWs." At the bottom of the cartoon, the caption read, "Which has the most power?"

Do you believe that prayer pays off personally? How does prayer benefit you as well as the people for whom you pray? What do we gain from a life of prayer?

I think that joy is one of the greatest blessings we receive from a life of prayer. Recall the words of Jesus: "Ask, and you will receive, that your joy may be full" (John 16:24 NKJV).

I love those words: "Your joy may be full." Again, we see the emphasis from Jesus that our prayers are heard in heaven. When God hears, he responds. And the result is fullness of joy for us.

I have yet to meet anyone who does not want to be happy.

Children love to laugh and overflow with delight. They seem to do it so naturally. As a grandfather, I notice that the younger grandkids thoroughly enjoy it when I tickle them or make funny faces or engage in silly antics. The older ones now need me to talk to them in a "more mature fashion," so I tell them corny jokes or give them riddles to solve. But regardless of age, they all like to be "full of joy" and laughter.

This is a phrase that John obviously learned from Jesus:

> *That which we have seen and heard we declare to you, that you also may have fellowship with us; and truly our fellowship is with the Father and with His Son Jesus Christ. And these things we write to you* that your joy may be full *(1 John 1:3–4* NKJV, *emphasis added).*

Do you see how John used the same words as Jesus? In his writings, he tells us that he was an eyewitness to the ministry of Jesus and that he heard firsthand the words of Jesus. He tells us that the purpose of his words is to bring us into fellowship with the apostles through their writings, and that their fellowship was truly with Jesus. If we grow through prayer and study of the Scriptures, we will ultimately fellowship with the Lord.

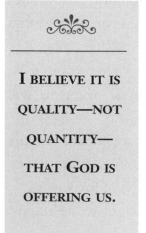

I BELIEVE IT IS QUALITY—NOT QUANTITY—THAT GOD IS OFFERING US.

The point is not that we can be *filled with joy*, but that our *joy may be full*. Does that sound like hair-splitting? I believe it is quality—not quantity—that God is offering us. When it comes to prayer paying off personally, we receive a deep-down kind of joy that is far beyond that which comes from buying a new luxury car or a five-bedroom house on ten acres of land. It is rich and everlasting joy that God brings to us.

The apostle Paul said: "If we have food and clothing, we will be content with that" (1 Tim. 6:8). In our society, with its wealth and free-enterprise system, we can work to obtain nearly anything. If the material world has a draw for us, then we can work hard and accumulate all kinds of toys and luxuries. But in societies with more oppressive forms of rule and less abundance, acquiring "goodies" is not even an option. Christians in that kind of situation are free to pray because they *love God*, not because they view prayer as a catalog to present to the "great Santa Claus" in the sky.

The bottom line is this: Prayer really does pay off for us personally, but it depends largely on what payoff we are expecting. If we are expecting a new car, a new house, a new wardrobe, and other such new "stuff," we may not get that kind of payoff. But if we are expecting joy and contentment, we can count on those things.

Praying as a Parent

Another big payoff for those who dedicate themselves to prayer concerns family members. Sandy and I raised five children on a fairly meager salary for many years. We were not focused on anything other than a roof over our heads, good health, and a car that would get us where we were going. We had no savings account or investments to trust in. We had our deep love for each other and five wonderful blessings from heaven.

The psalmist was absolutely right when he said, "Sons are a heritage from the LORD, children a reward from him. ... Blessed is the man whose quiver is full of them" (Ps. 127:3, 5).

As a young father, I learned from this Bible verse that our children were the Lord's, and we were their custodians. We were rewarded as parents with the opportunity to oversee their growth and development, both physically and spiritually. (Though there were times I was sure the psalmist meant that parents would quiver—and tremble and shudder—as they struggled to raise kids!)

From the time each of our children was born until their last evening in our house, I always laid hands on them individually and prayed for them. Every night that I was in town, I would pray beside them. If I came home late in the evening, I would quietly go into their rooms, lay my hand on their heads, and say a blessing for them. Even when they were teenagers, we still prayed together.

When I prayed for them, there were specific things that I asked God to do in their lives. One of these was, "God, bless my son or daughter." That may not sound specific, and it may even seem like one of those routine "God, bless this food" kind of prayers. But I was, in fact, asking for God's blessing, his favor and goodness, to be showered upon my children. I wanted the blessings of God to be on their young lives so that when they grew up and left home, those blessings would continue to follow them.

I always wanted them to serve the Lord, so I made that part of my prayer for them: "God, prepare this child to serve you when he/she grows up."

Another specific area of prayer that I learned from Sandy was to pray that God would be preparing their future husbands and wives—that God would be gracious to them and would lead them to marry people who loved him. Looking even farther into the future, I prayed for God to bless their children, my grandchildren, when the time came for them to raise a family. And a major prayer was asking God to keep them from the snares of the devil.

For many years, after the kids would take their baths, do their homework, and get into bed, Sandy and I would hear music to our

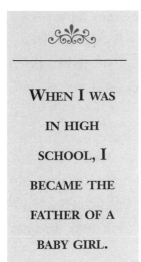

WHEN I WAS IN HIGH SCHOOL, I BECAME THE FATHER OF A BABY GIRL.

ears from each and every bedroom: "Mom, Dad, come and pray for me." This continued until they moved away and started their own families.

Praying as a Grandparent

I am no longer "Daddy"; now I am "Boppa." That is what our children called Sandy's father, so it was a real privilege for me to take on that name after he passed away and my children began to have their own children. Now here I am with thirteen beautiful grandchildren, and I see God's hand all the way back to my prayer legacy in Grandma Ella through my mother to me and my children and now my grandchildren.

When I was in high school, I became the father of a baby girl. Though I never saw that baby because she was immediately adopted from the hospital, we were able to find each other several years ago. Her name is Joy, and she is indeed a joy. Her parents, now retired, were in the ministry for many years. Joy is the mother of four wonderful girls, and when we found each other, she made me an instant grandfather before the children Sandy and I had began to have kids of their own.

Joy's daughter Whitney, who today is fifteen, was three years old when I first met her. It was my first meeting with Joy and her family, and we talked on into the night. When Whitney and her older sister, Tara, went to bed, I asked Joy if she would mind if I went in and prayed with the girls. No problem, she said. Joy is a Christian, and her little girls went to Sunday school and knew about prayer. So I knelt beside the little bed they shared. A cassette player on the nightstand softly played praise music to lull them to sleep.

I said, "Girls, as your grandfather, I would like to say a prayer for you just as I do for my children every night before they go to sleep."

So I put my hand on Whitney's forehead and started to pray. Whitney looked up at me and, in her three-year-old voice, said, "Hey, what do you think you're doing?"

"I'm going to bless you," I replied.

She said, "Go to your own house and bless yourself!"

Today, this fifteen-year-old beauty and her seventeen-year-old sister are both doing well in school and both are on the swim team and water polo team. Both of them, along with their two younger sisters, know and love Jesus.

Leaving a Prayer Legacy

Prayer is like a savings account at the bank. As you keep making deposits, the return keeps getting bigger and bigger, and it will be there for you years from now. I can assure you that as you pray for your family, you will reap great rewards as the years go by.

I did not have a father to teach me to pray. My father was an alcoholic until he died. I learned to pray from my heavenly Father, and he assured me that prayer would personally pay off. And it has done so in my life and in the life of my beautiful wife and our wonderful children. The legacy of prayer is ongoing for those who seek the Lord.

The Old Testament tells us about Job, who was "blameless and upright" and who "feared God and shunned evil" (Job 1:1). We also learn that he had seven sons and three daughters, and that he was quite wealthy: "He owned seven thousand sheep, three thousand camels, five hundred yoke of oxen and five hundred donkeys, and had a large number of servants." Indeed, Job was "the greatest man among all the people of the East" (Job 1:3). Here is the part I really like:

His sons used to take turns holding feasts in their homes, and they would invite their three sisters to eat and drink with them. When a period of feasting had run its course, Job would send and have them purified. Early in the morning he would sacrifice a burnt offering for each of them, thinking "Perhaps my children have sinned and cursed God in their hearts." This was Job's regular custom (Job 1:4–5).

I find this brief passage beautiful. Here is a story of one of the greatest men in history, and he sought the Lord on behalf of his children. He was concerned about the purity of his children's hearts, and so he made regular sacrifices to God in their stead.

How I urge you to see that prayer pays off personally when you seek God on behalf of your family! God will work through people who seek him on a regular basis. (We will talk much more about leaving a legacy of prayer in chapter 12.)

Body, Soul, and Spirit

In his writings to the church of the first century, Paul made a wonderful statement that opens up many new avenues of thought for us: "May God himself, the God of peace, sanctify you through and through. May your whole spirit, soul and body be kept blameless at the coming of our Lord Jesus Christ" (1 Thess. 5:23). The apostle reminds us that we are three-dimensional creatures. God is three-dimensional or, as it is often expressed, he is a Triune Being. He is Father, Son, and Holy Spirit. The baptism of Jesus helps to clarify this concept of the Holy Trinity:

As soon as Jesus was baptized, he went up out of the water. At that moment heaven was opened, and he saw the Spirit of God descending like a dove and lighting on him. And a voice from heaven said, "This is my Son, whom I love; with him I am well pleased" (Matt. 3:16–17).

Here we see God the Son rising from the Jordan River, God the Holy Spirit coming upon him like a dove, and God the Father speaking from heaven. That's quite incredible—a convergence of all three aspects of God.

You and I are also triune beings in the sense that we have a body, soul, and spirit, just as Paul said. The apostle John also shows us a glimpse into our multidimensional nature when he writes, "Beloved, I pray that you may prosper in all things and be in health, just as your soul prospers" (3 John 2 NKJV). He reminds us that we have a body that can be healthy and a soul that can be healthy. So when we think about how prayer pays off personally, we can be sure that it benefits us in the three aspects of our being—physically, mentally, and spiritually.

The Ministry of Jesus

The Gospel of Matthew gives us this glimpse of Jesus' ministry:

Jesus went throughout Galilee, teaching in their synagogues, preaching the good news of the kingdom, and healing every disease and sickness among the people. News about him spread all over Syria, and people brought to him all who were ill with various diseases, those suffering severe pain, the demon-possessed, those having seizures, and the paralyzed, and he healed them (Matt. 4:23–24).

Jesus worked with the body, soul, and spirit: challenging and defeating demons that possessed people, healing and cleansing disease and sickness, and healing those with mental infirmity. This was a great benefit for all of humanity. And please take note that the Gospel and healing were not just for "church people." Jesus is for *all* people, and he offers love and healing to everyone. That is why he said:

> *"Come to me, all you who are weary and burdened, and I will give you rest. Take my yoke upon you and learn from me, for I am gentle and humble in heart, and you will find rest for your souls. For my yoke is easy and my burden is light"* (Matt. 11:28–30).

THE LORD HEARS YOU AND WILL GIVE YOU REST AS YOU NEED IT.

The world is tired and weary, and the people of planet earth are heavy laden with many burdens. Jesus stands through the centuries with his arms outstretched promising to give rest to all people everywhere. You can find this rest for yourself through prayer. The Lord hears you and will give you rest as you need it. Now that, my friend, is a great payoff.

Good for the Soul

The human soul is one of God's most amazing creations. In Hebrew the word for *soul* is *nephesh,* while the Greek word is *psuche* or *psyche.* In both the Old and New Testaments, the soul is the seat of the emotions—it is "who we are." Thus it came to stand for the individual, the person, or the personal life. (Vine 1996)

149

The psalmist lets us know there is value to the human soul that money cannot buy. He also teaches that our soul can go on into eternity with God.

> *Those who trust in their wealth and boast in the multitude of their riches, none of them can by any means redeem his brother, nor give to God a ransom for him—for the redemption of their souls is costly, and it shall cease forever—that he should continue to live eternally, and not see the Pit (Ps. 49:6–9 NKJV).*

A few verses later, the psalmist states, "God will redeem my soul from the power of the grave, for He shall receive me" (Ps. 49:15 NKJV). Though hell would like to take my soul down into its very depths, God has the power to redeem my soul. I am in awe of God because of his forgiveness and his wonderful grace toward me. For many years, I allowed the world, the flesh, and the devil to dirty my soul and clog it with things that kept me from the love of God. I thank him for redeeming me from the power of death that would ultimately have taken my soul.

The human soul comes under spiritual attack, and when the soul is out of synch with God, it becomes distressed, as the psalmist states to the Lord:

> *For day and night Your hand was heavy upon me; my vitality was turned into the drought of summer (Ps. 32:4 NKJV).*

In our fast-paced society, we have seen a tremendous rise in stress and anxiety. In the United States, billions of dollars are spent on anti-depressants and anti-anxiety drugs that help replenish the natural serotonin that our brains need to give us a feeling of well-being. Yet we can turn to the Scriptures and find that God will heal our weary souls if we will just seek him:

> *Why are you downcast, O my soul? Why so disturbed*
> *within me? Put your hope in God, for I will yet praise him,*
> *my Savior and my God (Ps. 42:11).*

If I were your doctor, and you came to me for advice on how to handle stress and anxiety, I would give you a prescription to pray more and to read more of God's Word so that you would find peace.

In conclusion, the psalmist cries out to God: "My soul melts from heaviness; strengthen me according to Your word" (Ps. 119:28 NKJV). How simple it is to see the payoff we personally receive from prayer when we balance it with the Holy Scriptures. Our souls can be filled with the violence and turmoil of television, or they can be filled with the love and grace of our God. We get to choose how to handle the stress of our souls.

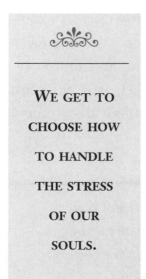

WE GET TO CHOOSE HOW TO HANDLE THE STRESS OF OUR SOULS.

Many times people lose their way in life simply because there is no light in their soul. God can fill your soul with light, and that light will shine positive thoughts into a distressed soul. As you fall in love with prayer, God's Holy Spirit will fill you to overflowing with the rest and peace your soul needs and desires. Do not let the pressures of life beat you down until you think you are worthless and invaluable. That is a lie of the devil. Jesus gives each of us this reassurance:

"Are not two sparrows sold for a penny? Yet not one of them will fall to the ground apart from the will of your Father. And even the very hairs of your head are numbered. So don't be afraid; you are worth more than many sparrows" (Matt. 10:29–31).

Do not lose sight of the fact that God has his eyes on the sparrow, and if that is so, how much more are his eyes on you!

Good for the Spirit

Our spirit is able to communicate with God's Spirit like no other part of us. When we pray, our spirit is able to respond to the will of God, so that we can grow spiritually. Prayer allows our spirit to soar like an eagle high above the beautiful firs of the pristine Alaskan forests.

The apostle Paul had much to say to the early Christian community concerning the soul and the spirit of man. Often we feel a tugging in our hearts or a reaction to some situation, and we cannot discern what it is that we are feeling. Often it is our spirit struggling within us. With prayer, we can hone our discernment and sharpen our spiritual skills.

The Spirit searches all things, even the deep things of God. For who among men knows the thoughts of a man except the man's spirit within him? In the same way no one knows the thoughts of God except the Spirit of God. We have not received the spirit of the world but the Spirit who is from God, that we may understand what God has freely given us. This is what we speak, not in words taught us by human wisdom but in words taught by the Spirit, expressing spiritual truths in spiritual words (1 Cor. 2:10–13).

Can you see how important it is to fall in love with prayer? There are two languages being spoken in, around, and through us. We have two competing languages at work: One is a worldly language that confuses our soul, and the other is a spiritual language that liberates our soul even as it brings self-control to our bodies.

James reminds us that our spirit is what keeps us going. Television commercials and magazine and newspaper ads all make us think that life is all about our bodies. Everything is offered to us with emphasis on how pleasing it is to the eyes, how it will make us look to others, how it can better our lot in life. Yet, in reality, we are "lost" without our spirit inhabiting and directing our body.

Since that is the truth, why do we spend so much time pampering and protecting our bodies while filling our souls with sludge and doing little or nothing to strengthen our spirits? As James says succinctly, "For as the body without the spirit is dead, so faith without works is dead also" (James 2:26 NKJV).

Invest in Prayer

If we look at prayer in a very practical way, we can find a comparison in the business world. If we invest our money in the stock market or a business or a bank account, we are looking for a payoff. We want to make a return on our money. In the same manner, if we look at our prayer life as an investment, then we anticipate a payoff that brings an eternal return. Jesus told a parable that explains this principle:

He said therefore, "A certain nobleman went into a far country to receive for himself a kingdom, and to return.

*And he called his ten servants, and delivered them ten
pounds, and said unto them, Occupy till I come" (Luke
19:12–13 KJV).*

The word *occupy* here literally means to do business or to conduct affairs in a businesslike manner. If we are to occupy our
world, our neighborhoods, our schools, our businesses, our
homes, and our very lives, then we need to do so in a businesslike
manner. What is it that we are looking for in business? We are
looking for a return on our investment. We want to make a profit
at the end of the year.

In the same way, we need to have a profitable *life,* and to do
that we need to invest our time wisely in prayer. At the end, when
all is said and done and our lives are accounted for in heaven, the
question will be: Did we get a payoff or receive a return for our
times of prayer?

The Blessings of Prayer

When I gave my heart to God, Sandy and I were divorced. There
was not a chance in Las Vegas that we would ever be together
again. However, I had an early discipline in prayer that helped us
"beat the odds." I attended our men's prayer meeting every
Saturday night. I sat in the sanctuary with three hundred other
men and prayed from 7:00 P.M. to 9:00 P.M.

For a man who loved to party on Saturday nights, this must
have raised some angelic eyebrows in heaven, to say the least.
Only God could have captured my heart and imagination to make
prayer look exciting and worthwhile.

Every week for a month, I prayed for Sandy and our two children. My prayers for each were direct and straightforward: "Please,
God, save their souls." Little did I know that in less than six weeks,

WHEN I GAVE MY HEART TO GOD, SANDY AND I WERE DIVORCED. THERE WAS NOT A CHANCE IN LAS VEGAS THAT WE WOULD EVER BE TOGETHER AGAIN.

God would win Sandy's heart, and she would surrender her life to him. Nor did I have the slightest inclination that we would be remarried in ten months, after almost three years of divorce. Are there rewards that flow from a praying life? My wife and I, along with our children and grandchildren, answer with a resounding, "Yes!"

Remember, prayer is not an earthly work; it is a blessing from heaven. Deposit this truth deeply in your heart: So valuable are your prayers that angels are dispatched from heaven to receive and respond to them. They take them into the throne room of God Almighty, in beautiful golden bowls, where they are released into God's nostrils as sweet fragrant incense (see Rev. 8:1–4). Your heavenly Father loves it when you pray.

CHAPTER ELEVEN

THE ETERNAL VALUE OF PRAYER

"I have been driven many times to my knees by the overwhelming conviction that I had absolutely no other place to go."
ABRAHAM LINCOLN

We may be tempted to think of prayer only in terms of "here and now." We want God to heal our sick child. We want him to provide us a job. We want him to mend our broken relationships. The Lord does, indeed, meet us right where we are, and he is concerned about our daily needs and desires.

But prayer goes far beyond our everyday lives here on planet earth. Our prayers stretch on into eternity, and, in a very real sense, they have value and significance in ways we can hardly fathom. How can our prayers affect eternity? How can we have an eternal impact on other people?

The great writer and Christian leader Dorothy Sayers once said: "It is precisely because of the eternity outside of time that everything in time becomes valuable and important and meaningful. Therefore, Christianity makes it of urgent importance that everything we do here should be rightly related to what we eternally are. 'Eternal life' is the sole sanction for the values of this life." (Sayers 1998)

As we have done in previous chapters, let's look at Jesus as our example. This chapter will revolve around Jesus' prayer in John 17, where he is preparing his disciples for his departure from the earth.

Referring to himself, he says to his heavenly Father, "You granted him authority over all people that he might give eternal life to all those you have given him" (John 17:2). People are noth-

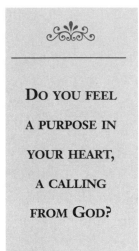

DO YOU FEEL A PURPOSE IN YOUR HEART, A CALLING FROM GOD?

ing but clay pots; we are jars of clay (see 2 Cor. 4:7). You and I are made out of the same elements from which the earth is made. But Jesus had the authority from God to come down here and give to you and me eternal life. That was his mission, and he knew that if he completed that mission, he would glorify God.

What is your mission? Are you headed in a specific direction? Do you feel a purpose in your heart, a calling from God?

Jesus' mission was inextricably linked to eternity. He said that the Son would glorify the Father by offering eternal life to those who were given to him. That is a powerful message for us too: Whatever our mission in life, it should encompass an eternal perspective. It should reach beyond this world and extend into the world to come.

As we look at Jesus' words, we realize that there is eternal value to prayer. It doesn't just start and end like a telephone conversation. It is ongoing and long-lasting. That's why the book of Revelation says that the prayers of the saints are like a fragrance; they rise up, and the angels carry them to God's throne in golden vials. They are handed to him, and he smells the fragrance of all the prayers that come up before him (see Rev. 8:3–4). So there is an eternal value to prayer because God dwells in an eternal realm, where there are no time constraints or limitations.

That is really fantastic. Think about it. You and I live in a certain time zone, and we use words such as *seconds, minutes,* and *hours* to describe this moment in which we live. Our language binds us to time—past, present, future. That is the realm in which we pray.

Yet our prayers somehow leave this realm and penetrate a spiritual dimension that stretches from eternity past to eternity future. They are heard by the Creator of both dimensions, and he responds in a timeless dimension and sends back an answer into this time zone.

We are sometimes astounded by space exploration—and rightly so. NASA sends up probes and spacecraft that transmit messages from light years away. The more amazing thing is, you and I can communicate directly with the Creator who watches over all the planets. The Old Testament prophet Nehemiah wrote of God, "You alone are the LORD. You made the heavens, even the highest heavens, all their starry host, the earth and all that is on it" (Neh. 9:6). And it was Moses who said to the people of God that God "rides on the heavens to help you" (Deut. 33:26). This is phenomenal.

Seeing Beyond the Here and Now

Some people have a hard time grasping the concept of *eternal* life. That's because everything in our culture emphasizes the short-term, the tangible, the immediate. We go for what's right in front of us. If we can see it, smell it, taste it, touch it, and hear it, *then* we will believe it's real. If we have to look into the future, if something is way off in the distance, it becomes abstract and vague to us.

We are like the Children of Israel in the wilderness. They kept hearing about a great place called the Promised Land. They had been told they would have wells they hadn't dug, orchards they hadn't planted, homes they hadn't built. It would be a land of "milk and honey." That sounded incredible. But in the meantime, they were dealing with short-term problems and discomforts: blisters on their feet, pebbles in their sandals; the scorching sun beating down on them.

They grumbled, complained, and worried about themselves, about what they were going to eat, what they were going to drink, and what they were going to wear. God even chided them about it, saying, "Didn't I give you shoes in the wilderness that never wore out?" (see Deut. 29:5). Now think of that. They each were given a pair of shoes that lasted for forty years. One pair. God provides for his children, but we always have to have more to appease the flesh.

WE BECOME SO FOCUSED ON OUR NEEDS RIGHT NOW—ALL OF THE DAILY NITTY-GRITTY—THAT WE FORGET ABOUT THE PROMISED LAND TOWARD WHICH WE ARE HEADED.

God also said to them, "Didn't I give you manna? But you didn't want angel's food" (see Deut. 8:3,16). So they grumbled about how God fed them. He said, "You want meat? Okay, I'll give you meat." The next morning they woke up to a swarm of quail flying into the camp. Soon they had quail stew, quail sandwiches, and quail burgers. They had diced quail, sliced quail, and sautéed quail. In fact, the Bible is very specific about it—they had so much meat that it started coming out of their noses (see Num. 11:23).

Don't we have that same attitude sometimes? We become so focused on our needs right now—all of the daily nitty-gritty—that we forget about the Promised Land toward which we are headed. Pray for your everyday needs, for they are indeed significant to God, but pray also with an eye toward eternity.

Eternal Life Defined

In his priestly prayer to his heavenly Father, Jesus said that he had been granted authority by God to give to us eternal life, but what does that mean exactly? As Jesus moved on in his prayer, he defined eternal life: "Now this is eternal life: that they may know you, the only true God, and Jesus Christ, whom you have sent" (John 17:3). That's pretty straightforward. Eternal life is given to us so that we may know God.

The Greek word translated *know* sometimes means to "understand through experience."[2] When you have given your heart to God and have come to know him by experience, you have been born again. You have the assurance of eternal life. So to know God, to truly *know* him, to experience him personally, means that God is in control of your life and that he is living in you. It is not a matter of singing about him and talking about him in a theoretical way. You *know* him. And you seek to know his purpose for your life and how he wants to work through you to influence eternity.

Mission Accomplished

Jesus went on to say in his prayer to the Father, "I have brought you glory on earth by completing the work you gave me to do. And now, Father, glorify me in your presence with the glory I had with you before the world began" (John 17:4–5).

If you were to die right now and go to heaven, could you honestly say to God, "I completed my mission, and I glorified you, Father. I fulfilled the purpose you gave to me"?

I will never forget what Billy Graham said to David Frost during an interview a few years ago. Frost said, "Billy, you know you are so admired and so praised and so loved, and people speak so well of you. You've had such a great relationship with the media, with the whole world. Very seldom are there many negative things said about you. How do you handle all this praise?"

Billy Graham replied, "Well, David, I don't listen to the praise. There's only one thing that I want to hear, and that's from my Lord Jesus Christ: 'Well done, good and faithful servant.' I'm not sure I will hear that, but that's what I want to hear." If Billy Graham is not sure, where does that leave the rest of us? I have been with him on the platform when he has been sitting there struggling with the effects of Parkinson's disease, his Bible shaking, his hands shaking and trembling. Then T. W. Wilson or George Beverly Shea or his son Ned or Franklin will reach over and say, "Here, let me help you." And with help, he will stand and walk, shaking a little bit, up to the pulpit. We may see him in this physical discomfort, but when he puts his hands on the pulpit, all of a sudden—boom—the shaking stops, and he is a young man again. He preaches the Gospel, and then when he is through, he walks back, sits down, and starts shaking again.

WHY DO I GET SO EASILY DISTRACTED? WHY DO I SPEND TIME ON THINGS THAT HAVE NO ETERNAL VALUE?

162

I have watched him in his suffering, and I don't know how he could *not* feel that Jesus is going to say to him, "Well done, good and faithful servant."

Thinking about the dedication and great work of Billy Graham makes me stop to evaluate my own activities. Why do I get so easily distracted? Why do I spend time on things that have no eternal value? Jesus said, "I have glorified you, Father." Here is a prayer that is very open, very honest. In it Jesus was giving a report, an account of himself to his Father.

Prayer involves accountability. We listen for God's direction and then, later, we tell him how we fared in accomplishing his plans for us. When we pray, we are acknowledging our accountability to the one who made us and gave us our mission.

Compassionate Prayers

In his prayer, Jesus continued giving an account of himself to God the Father: "I have revealed you to those whom you gave me out of the world. They were yours; you gave them to me and they have obeyed your word" (John 17:6). Even as he reported to the Father about his mission, Jesus spoke about his followers lovingly.

Jesus was praying for the disciples, who were right around him, listening in. Real, earnest, heartfelt prayer expresses love, warmth, passion, and compassion. Jesus was praying for his friends who were standing right there with him. That may have been the first time they had ever heard him acknowledge to God the Father that he had a purpose for them and that he had accomplished that purpose.

Do you have a prayer time like that, one in which your friends and family know that you are praying for them? Have they ever actually *heard* you pray for them? Do your children know that you are praying for their future? Have your sons and daughters actually *heard* you pray *for* them and *about* them? Do your children have the blessings of knowing that their father and mother are praying on their behalf?

That is what Jesus was showing us here in this prayer. Yes, it is a prayer of intercession, but it is also a prayer that is full of compassion and warmth. In it Jesus lifted up his eyes to heaven, and the people for whom he was praying were standing right there listening to what he said. How could it not overwhelm our heart if we overheard Jesus Christ praying for us? What if our best friend or our neighbor or our teacher or even our boss heard us praying for them?

We too can be a blessing to others as we pray for them with love and grace.

Prayer That Encourages

Imagine how you would have felt if you had been one of those disciples listening to Jesus pray. He told the Father, "Now they know that everything you have given me comes from you. For I gave them the words you gave me and they accepted them. They knew with certainty that I came from you, and they believed that you sent me" (John 17:7–8).

He was then reporting to the Father that everything was going as planned. And he was kind of bragging about these men: "They got it; I told them that I am the Messiah, the Son of the Living God, and they believed it."

Now imagine how those men must have felt realizing that God had a purpose for their lives, even though they weren't clear about it themselves. That is just like you and me. Many times we don't know what next year will bring or where we are headed in our marriage or what is going to happen with our finances when the property taxes come due. We have no idea why we are in our current job, when it seems so meaningless and mundane. God has a plan and a purpose, and our responsibility is to believe it and trust him to fulfill it.

Down here at ground level where we live, there is a seventy- or eighty-year period called life through which we are working our way. Life can be such a mystery. We learn it as we are experiencing it, and we keep thinking that everything in it is going to come together all of a sudden. We keep thinking that someday we are going to win the lottery or that Ed McMahon is going to knock on our door with that big cardboard check and say to us, "Congratulations! You are the winner!" We may think life is something else, but it is what we are doing while we are waiting for that something else to happen. And in waiting for something else, we miss life itself.

Imagine the feeling if you were standing there and heard Jesus talking to the Father about you: "This is so awesome. He/she heard about me and believed that I am the Son of God. I have a mission for him/her to accomplish on earth, but the most important part is already taken care of. He/she and I are going to spend eternity together."

Does that sound too good to be true? Well, that is exactly how the apostle Paul explained it: "Christ Jesus, who died—more than that, who was raised to life—is at the right hand of God and is also interceding for us" (Rom. 8:34). If that doesn't make you feel better about yourself, little else will.

But there is even more. Jesus went on to tell his Father, "I pray for ... those you have given me, for they are yours. All I have is yours, and all you have is mine. And glory has come to me through them" (John 17:9–10). Another translation of verse 10 says, "I am glorified in them" (NKJV).

Can Jesus be glorified in *us*? What a thought—that God's Son is glorified in you and me. That is a strong statement: He is

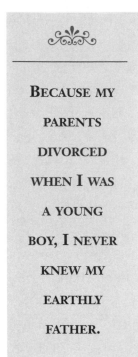

BECAUSE MY PARENTS DIVORCED WHEN I WAS A YOUNG BOY, I NEVER KNEW MY EARTHLY FATHER.

glorified in us. If we are men and women of prayer, we help release that glory, because our relationship with God gets stronger and stronger as we come to know him better and better.

Kept in His Name

Because my parents divorced when I was a young boy, I never knew my earthly father. But to know my heavenly Father, and to know that I am one of his children—that he cares about me , that he provides for me, that he looks after me, that he walks and talks with me—that is totally awesome!

This is the assurance that Jesus gave us when he prayed for us: "Holy Father, protect them by the power of your name—the name you gave me—so that they may be one as we are one. While I was with them, I protected them and kept them safe by that name you gave me" (John 17:11–12). That is a beautiful statement. When we commit ourselves to Christ as his followers and disciples, we share in the power of his name. When we claim the one true and living God as our Father, we are protected by his might and authority.

No matter how big a storm you may be facing, never doubt his presence. The disciples had learned to trust Jesus during a literal storm when the boat in which they were sailing started filling up with water (see Mark 4). They ran to Jesus and said, "Teacher, don't you care if we drown?" (v. 38). Of course he cared. If there is one thing that these men should have known from being with Jesus it is that he cared.

Was Jesus concerned about drowning? No. After all, he was the one who had said, "Let us go over to the other side" (v. 35). He knew he was going to make it. He was asleep in the back of the boat because he was exhausted (see v. 38), but he was at total peace in the midst of that storm.

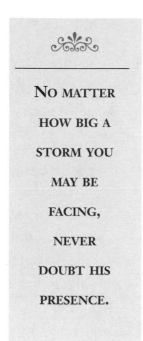

NO MATTER HOW BIG A STORM YOU MAY BE FACING, NEVER DOUBT HIS PRESENCE.

We should be grateful that Jesus is in this storm with us. We should say, "Let's see how he is going to work this out. What are you going to do, Jesus? I can see no way that we are going to make it through this storm, but with you on board I know it is going to be an adventure."

In his prayer, Jesus showed that the disciples had come a long way: "They believe that you sent me and they follow me now" (see John 17:8.) We can see spiritual growth in these men because of his prayer for them. It is beautiful when we stop and think what he said about them to his Father, "I have kept them in your name" (see v. 12).

How important it is to fall in love with the Bible and with prayer so that we fall in love with God. If we will take his Word and mix it with prayer, there is no storm that this world can throw at us that will ever win over us, because we know that he does care. We can go back to his Word and say, "Oh, that's right. He said, 'Let's go over to the other side.' He didn't say, 'Let's go part way and drown.' He is taking us through."

When the storms are raging, we really get close to him. When the sky is sunny and there are no problems, we feel no urgency to trust him. But when trouble comes, then we cling to him.

Life is full of sinking boats and storms and doubts and anxieties. But this is eternal life—that we know the only true God. He is in every storm with us, and his Son, Jesus Christ, cares deeply for us.

In Jesus' prayer for his disciples, he said to his Father, "My prayer is not that you take them out of the world but that you protect them from the evil one" (John 17:15). Jesus did not say that he would take us out of tough situations, but he will see us through to the other side.

Fall in Love with Prayer

Jesus reminded us again that this world, this place called earth, is not our home: "They are not of the world, even as I am not of it" (John 17:16). And so he emphasized once more that, although we are here for a purpose, one day we will move on to our permanent home.

How will we make it through our time here on earth, with its hardships and hassles, its defeats and disappointments? By remembering what Jesus said to his Father and ours, "Sanctify them by the truth; your word is truth" (John 17:17).

Earlier he said, "I have given them your word" (see v. 8). The message he delivered is true and trustworthy. Jesus felt that the Word of God was so important that he left his throne in glory and came down to earth to make it available to you and me. He died to deliver the message to us. That is how important the Scriptures were to the only begotten Son of God. We make a mockery of God by denying prayer and the Bible. And we will miss the life God intended for us if we are not men and women of prayer, men and women of the Bible.

I urge you to begin today to make prayer and Bible study a top priority in your life. You will find yourself falling in love with the

Bible and falling in love with prayer. And in the process you will fall in love with God himself.

As one of my heroes of the faith, Charles Spurgeon, once said, "Time is short. Eternity is long. It is only reasonable that this short life be lived in light of eternity." So true. And when you live in the light of eternity, you will naturally find yourself praying more and more.

As we have seen in this chapter, even Jesus, the unique Son of God, realized the tremendous importance of prayer not only in the here and now but also in the hereafter. He prayed not so much for himself as for others. We have seen how he prayed for his disciples in their presence in order to strengthen and encourage them and to set an example for them to follow in their own prayer life.

Jesus knew that a life of prayer does not end with the passing of the one who prays, but that it has an enduring effect upon the lives of those who follow. Prayer is a legacy that lives on for generations to come.

CHAPTER TWELVE

THE LEGACY OF PRAYER

"The main lesson about prayer is just this: Do it! Do it! Do it!"
JOHN LAIDLAW

My own love of prayer is a legacy handed down to me from other lovers of prayer. The cast of characters who have walked across the stage of my heart is wonderful. And each one of them built upon the prayer life of the person or persons who went before them.

The people I am going to introduce to you in this chapter had a number of things in common. They all loved God—he was central in their thinking and being—they all loved the Bible, they all loved people, they all loved to pray, and they all loved to laugh. This may not seem significant to you in the overall scheme of things, but it shows me that there is continuity in the life of prayer.

It is amazing how God weaves together circumstances and life paths to bring us blessings, often in unimaginable and miraculous ways. As you read the following stories, I encourage you to reflect on the people who influenced your own spiritual growth—and to consider how you might do the same for others.

Ella Olson: Never Give Up on Prayer
Ella Olson was born in 1886 to a wealthy businessman in North

Dakota named George Rose. George owned a bank and several other enterprises in his local area of Ellendale. He owned a large farm and homesteaded his property. It was this property that began his rise to prominence from a meager beginning to a place of respect among his neighbors.

He was one of the civic leaders of his community and was both a strict father and a shrewd businessman. This self-made man and his wife, Alice, had seven children, one of whom was Ella. She became a Christian at the age of seventeen, which went against the grain of the rest of her family. Ella was the only one in her family to become a Christian. It is said that the rest of the family mocked her for her young belief and faith in Jesus Christ.

Within the next two years, Ella fell in love with a young immigrant whose family had come from Ireland. Nineteen-year-old David Lane was, in Ella's eyes, a handsome man who was filled with God. David was an itinerant Methodist preacher who went from town to town throughout North Dakota. David and Ella were married and began their family together on a pittance of income.

David died at the young age of twenty-seven, leaving Ella and three children: George, Kenneth, and Ruth. Little did this young preacher know that he would have a grandson named after him who also would die an untimely death at the age of twenty-six.

Ella's father and family disowned Ella because she married a minister. There were two things her father strongly disliked: ministers and foreigners. He was a bigoted man, self-made and strong-willed, but he stood by his beliefs at all costs—even the cost of losing one of his own offspring. Ella had challenged that "golden calf" and had broken it by marrying the godly Irishman David Lane.

Ella was left alone without any money and with three children to raise on her own. She was smart, and with her education she was able to get a job as a teacher in a one-room school. So harsh was her life and existence as a single mom that her youngest son, Kenneth, died at the age of eleven. After surviving numerous tornadoes, freezing winters, and empty food cupboards, she packed up and moved to Oregon. There she established herself and her handsome son, George, and beautiful daughter, Ruth, in a new community and surroundings. And it was there that she would meet and marry a Norwegian Christian named Chris Olson.

George tolerated his mother's strict adherence to Christian principles while growing up, but he moved out of the house as soon as he could do so. His dear mother's aspirations were for him to become a preacher like his father before him. George Vernon Lane pursued a life of business, ultimately becoming a vice-president of the United States Gypsum Corporation. He married a beautiful Catholic woman named Marjory, and they raised five wonderful and successful children.

TRAGIC NEWS CAME TO RUTH ON A BEAUTIFUL, SUNNY AUGUST AFTERNOON.

Ruth went a different direction—she wanted to dance and have fun. This gregarious beauty loved people and enjoyed life. Everything was a challenge to her and an adventure for her. She was gifted with a free spirit and a zest for living. Her choices in life took her, like her brother George, away from her roots of faith in Jesus Christ and a life disciplined by the Scriptures in which she had been raised.

In her lifetime Ruth tripped and stumbled often with several failed marriages and heartbreak after heartbreak. Tragic news came to Ruth on a beautiful, sunny August afternoon. At the time she was living in Portland, Oregon, with two of her sons in a modest two-bedroom apartment on the second floor. She had just returned from a long day at work when a friend of the family came calling to bring heartbreaking news. It was August 19, 1959. Her oldest son, twenty-six-year-old David, had been killed in an automobile accident. This single mother was devastated, along with her remaining fifteen- and sixteen-year-old sons, Kent and Mike.

Both Kent and Mike made attempts during their remaining high school years to join the Christian Club and go to church. Each boy made a profession of faith in Jesus, but neither lived a life devoted to Jesus.

After years of heartache and struggle for this family, God intervened. Mike gave his heart to God at the age of twenty-six and found a great comfort in his faith and a calling from God on his life. If there was anyone who was delighted to hear of Mike's conversion, it was his grandmother Ella. Mike entered the ministry early in his Christian walk, and serving God was his top priority. Ella had seen thirty years of prayer answered for one of her wayward grandsons.

One day she asked Mike if he would conduct her funeral when she died. Ella Olson, as you may have guessed, was my grandmother. And the very first funeral service I ever conducted was hers.

Before she died, she said to me, "Michael, I have prayed for you all of your life, and God has answered my prayers. I have prayed for your mother and your brothers and all of my family for many years. Please promise me that you will go to your Uncle George and tell him the Gospel of Jesus Christ. He is lost and needs to find God again."

My mother, Ruth, had worked hard to care for her children, but by today's standards she would have been below the poverty line. Uncle George came to her rescue a couple of times with money when there was no food. Though I honestly didn't know him well, I feared him because he was a tall and large man. He was the epitome of a Fortune 500 businessman with a stern countenance. I kept my distance whenever he was around.

When Grandma died and I conducted her funeral, I figured I had fulfilled my obligation because Uncle George was in the front row during the ceremony. He had heard the Gospel, I reasoned. So I would not have to feel uncomfortable around him anymore.

THE STORY COULD END HERE, EXCEPT THAT GRANDMA ELLA'S PRAYERS WERE STILL WORKING.

That sure wasn't God's idea though. Two years later, Grandma Ella's sister died, and Uncle George asked me to officiate at the funeral. So I got to present the Gospel a second time to Uncle George. Looking back, I know that George was the kind of strong, domineering male figure that I was not used to, which is why I feared him. Having grown up without a father, I found Uncle George intimidating.

The story could end here, except that Grandma Ella's prayers were still working. She had known Jesus for seventy years, and her gift was for prayer, and specifically, intercessory prayer.

This woman, who had survived the death of two husbands and one child, abandonment by her father, harsh winters and boiling summers in North Dakota, and myriads of other trials and tribulations, was called by God Almighty to pray—and to pray for people who could not, or would not, pray for themselves. She wanted her son in heaven, and so she passed the torch to me.

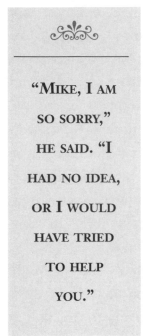

"MIKE, I AM SO SORRY," HE SAID. "I HAD NO IDEA, OR I WOULD HAVE TRIED TO HELP YOU."

Years later, when Uncle George was an old man, I called him and told him I was in his city of Altadena, California, not far from the famous Rose Bowl. He had just had eye surgery a few days earlier and was sitting alone in his big house. His children had all grown up and were out on their own. I asked if I could come over.

At first I was uncomfortable being in his house, and then as we sat and talked the tension disappeared. I realized that this man was just like everyone else, just a normal human being trying his best to live a happy life. The trophies of corporate America didn't matter anymore. Time had caught up with him, and he looked very vulnerable.

He said, "Mike, your mother told me that you had a problem with drugs and alcohol as a young man and that you overcame that."

"Yes, sir, I did," I replied.

"Mike, I am so sorry," he said. "I had no idea, or I would have tried to help you."

That comment changed all of my childhood misconceptions of the rich uncle who had never helped.

"How did you do it, Mike? I hear that you are now a minister and that you have a wonderful family and are doing well."

I explained how, as a little boy, I met Jesus in a Baptist church in Portland, Oregon, but that later, as a teenager, I had rebelled and gone on my own path until recent years. He sat in the dimly lit family room behind his dark prescription glasses looking toward me intently. Then I told him how I had prayed and asked God to forgive me of my sins and to give me another chance with my life. And I shared how the Holy Spirit had healed me from all my heartache and loneliness, and had actually delivered me from the abuse of drugs and alcohol.

Amazing, I thought. *I have given Uncle George the Gospel three times now.*

He paused and said, "You know, your grandmother loved you and prayed for you and your brothers. It broke her heart when your brother David was killed in that auto accident. Your mother and I always had a hard time with our mother because she was so religious and wanted us to be religious. I could never understand it. But now I can see that something wonderful has happened to you and that you are becoming successful without any background or training."

When I left his house, I thanked the Lord that many childhood hurts had been dealt with and resolved. Over the next few years, Uncle George would come to visit and take Sandy and me to dinner occasionally. It was a pleasant relationship. I appreciated him, not as the rich uncle I had always feared and avoided; and he appreciated me, not as the poor kid of a rebellious sister.

Then another surprise occurred. I couldn't believe the phone call I received from Uncle George asking me to meet him halfway between Los Angeles and San Diego. We sat in a restaurant in San Clemente where we met for lunch, just talking about our families. Then as dessert was served, he said, "Michael, Grandma used to tell me about being born again. Do you know what that means? Could you please explain it to me?"

My heart stopped, and my brain froze. *Was this really happening?* I thought. I began in chapter 3 of the Gospel of John and explained that Jesus said, "Unless one is born again, he cannot see the kingdom of God" (see v. 3).

"Well," he said, "I am an old man. How could I be born again?"

I gently told him that it takes faith at any age to simply believe and receive God's forgiveness of sins.

Once he heard the story and my explanation, he said, "Mike, would you mind telling me this one more time and quoting those Bible verses for me?" At which point, the brilliant, retired businessman from the highest levels of "big business" reached into his jacket pocket and pulled out a nice pen and a writing pad.

For the next thirty minutes, I went over the Scriptures and the simple steps to receive eternal life through faith in Jesus Christ. He very meticulously wrote down each important text and concept with the avid attention of a seminary student taking notes for his final exam. Uncle George died two weeks later from a massive heart attack. That wasn't the only miracle. My mother, Ruth, saw the change in my life and gave her heart to the Lord at the age of sixty. It is a full-blown miracle for anyone in that age group to surrender his or her life to Jesus. In fact, statistics tell us that the majority of Christians make their decision for Christ when they are in their teens. My mother told me that she had read the Bible every night before she went to bed from 1932 until 1972, when she was born again, and that until that moment she had never really known Jesus.

Ella Olson's prayers were still being answered.

As of this writing, my mother is eighty-nine years old and rises at four o'clock each morning to begin her prayers. The early rising is a covenant she made with God. She begins her time praying for her two sons, their families, and her many grandchildren and great-grandchildren. Jokingly, she said as Sandy and I celebrated the birth of two new grandsons: "Don't your children believe in birth control? Now I have to get up ten minutes earlier each morning to pray."

My mother has been handed the baton from *her* mother to be an intercessory prayer warrior. She has trained many people to pray and has groups of people praying at all times for our church and ministry. If any of the people of our church or the kids in our school need anything done, they know what to do: "Go pray with Ruth!"

Epilogue: Uncle George gave me a teddy bear for Christmas when I was two. His name is Brown Bear, and he sits in my den on my bookshelves with one eye missing, his nose stitched on, and most of his fur rubbed off from fifty-six years of being hugged by kids. He reminds me that a mother's prayers never fail, and that God hears the cries of a mother for her children's salvation.

One night in Palm Springs many years ago, I had finished speaking to a crowd in a hotel ballroom. An elderly lady approached me and said, "Michael, did you grow up in Oregon? Did you have a grandmother named Ella Olson?"

I answered this dear old saint that she was indeed right on both counts.

"Well," she said, "I was a friend of your grandmother and attended the Eugene Nazarene Church with her. On Wednesdays she held a prayer meeting in her house for the women of the church. And that grandmother of yours could pray the shingles off the roof!"

For Ella Olson, there could be no higher compliment.

W. J. Willis: Go Beyond "Ordinary" Prayers

W. J. Willis was saved in 1905 at the age of fifteen. He was sitting all alone in the balcony of a small Baptist church in Great Britain; he heard the Gospel of Jesus Christ and gave his heart to the Lord that day.

Mr. Willis, as all of us who loved him called him, was saved during the famous Welsh Revival. This was a phenomenal time in history, when the power of God moved so strongly in Wales that coal miners came up from the pits with tears streaming down their soot-darkened faces. Brothels went out of business, taverns were closed, and churches were open around the clock, filled with people weeping and crying out to God for their sins. It was a supernatural collision of two civilizations: the kingdom of God and the kingdom of this world were meeting face to face.

There was a young man named Evan Roberts, whom God used in a mighty way. Though Evan would not have been called the leader of the revival, he was in the forefront of it. This young man and his brother led prayer meetings all over Wales, and God used him as a catalyst for the revival. He was so humble that when he was invited to speak at a church, he would consent to do so only if the pastor agreed upon two conditions. The first was that the pastor would not tell the congregation that Evan was coming, and the second was that the pastor would not tell Evan the date. Only God could bring the audience, and only God could lead Evan step by step and day by day.

"I SAY TO YOU TONIGHT, ORDINARY PRAYER WILL NOT WORK!"

Time and again, when Evan would arrive at a church meeting which he felt he should attend, the facility would be full of people. Sometimes the Holy Spirit of God was so prevalent that Evan would sit in the audience for hours and cry and laugh and sing with the people. At such times, he would not get up to speak, nor would he reveal to anyone that he was there. Other times he would walk out onto the stage, and the Spirit of God would fall on the crowd; he would just sit there on a chair and cry and pray because of the conviction of God's Spirit.

This is the environment that Mr. Willis grew up in as young teenager. He was a close friend of Evan's brother, and he was greatly influenced by the move of God at that time. Mr. Willis went on to study at Spurgeon's Pastor College, and then went to Cardiff and taught at the school of Rees Howells. (If you have never read the book *Rees Howells: Intercessor* by Norman Percy Grubb, it is a must for your library.)

Fast forward to 1973. As the director of a new Christian music ministry named Maranatha! Music, I had just taken delivery of the very first praise album we had produced. It began a series of praise albums and CDs that have circled the globe. That day I heard the Holy Spirit say to me, "Take three hundred albums with you tonight and give them as gifts from God, and I will bless this music and Maranatha! Music."

That evening I had been invited by my good friend Doug Sutphen to attend a special dinner in an exclusive neighborhood of Los Angeles. Doug has a huge heart for China and was burdened for the spiritual lives of the Chinese people. Many wealthy and famous people would be in attendance at this dinner. There would be a Chinese meal served to all of the guests, and a young man from mainland China would be speaking. This was a novelty because China at that time was a closed country, and not many Americans were traveling there, nor were many Chinese people coming to America. This Chinese Christian was going to speak to the crowd about the church in China and the need for Bibles in that country.

My grandmother had been an intercessory prayer warrior for the people of China since she was a young woman. My mother told me not many years ago that my grandmother would travail over China in prayer although she had never seen a Chinese person when she lived in North Dakota in the early 1900s. I was fascinated by this dinner invitation and took the free recordings as God had instructed. I never dreamed that my life would forever be changed.

After dinner, there was some special music by Chuck Girard, and then Doug introduced the young man who was to speak. We were all mesmerized by the tales he told of the growing home churches and the persecution that many Christians endured in China.

At the conclusion of his talk, Doug closed by saying, "And now we must commit this great need to prayer before God's throne." At which time he introduced Mr. W. J. Willis. Mr. Willis walked to the front of the crowded entertainment room of this beautiful mansion. He was all of five feet tall, weighed maybe a hundred pounds dripping wet, and was dressed in a black suit with a clerical collar. His white hair was neatly combed back, his wispy white mustache perfectly trimmed, and his perfectly shined wingtips were spotless. He was the image of the perfect English gentleman.

Mr. Willis reached into his pocket and pulled out a small Bible and thumped it on his hand. Then, staring everyone directly in the eye, he said with a voice the volume of three men larger than himself, "Ordinary prayer will not work for China, or for these men who are willing to see that the church gets Bibles."

What? I said to myself. *What does he mean by that?*

Then he said again as he thumped his little leather pocket Bible on his open palm, "I say to you tonight, ordinary prayer will not work!"

That's it, I thought. *If this little whippersnapper says that one more time, I am going to stand up and rebuke him. Ordinary prayer always works. The Bible says so. I pray, and it always works.*

Then he had the nerve to say a third time, "Ordinary prayer will not work!"

As I began to rise from my chair, he said, "Turn in your Bibles to 1 Timothy 2."

He began to read the first three verses in the *New King James Version*: "Therefore I exhort first of all that supplications, prayers, intercessions, and giving of thanks be made for all men, for kings and all who are in authority, that we may lead a quiet and peaceable life in all godliness and reverence. For this is good and acceptable in the sight of God our Savior."

It was here that my understanding was opened to a new dimension and understanding of prayer and the importance of praying for others. Mr. Willis placed his emphasis on the word *intercessions*. To him, this was beyond the "normal" everyday prayers we may make to the Lord. This eighty-six-year-old gentleman introduced me to the realm of intercessory prayer. He had learned as a missionary to Korea in the 1920s and 1930s to intercede for a people who were without Jesus. To this man and to my grandmother and to my mother, intercessory prayer was a call from God—a heavenly call by which God "gifted" people with a burden on their hearts to pray for other people.

Technically, I don't think there is such a thing as "normal" or "ordinary" prayer, because prayer is so abnormal for our flesh and extraordinary from our earthly perspective. There actually is

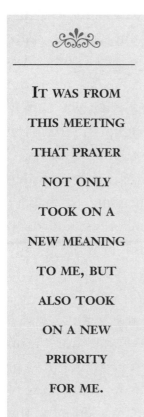

IT WAS FROM THIS MEETING THAT PRAYER NOT ONLY TOOK ON A NEW MEANING TO ME, BUT ALSO TOOK ON A NEW PRIORITY FOR ME.

nothing normal in the human realm about prayer. It is a gift from God to his creatures, one that he has given to us to communicate with him.

But I want to put an emphasis on the great experience that awaits us, and the impact we can have on others, when we become people who not only pray for ourselves, but also are willing to spend our time praying for others. It probably would be safe to say that our love for anyone can be measured by how we pray for that person.

It was from this meeting that prayer not only took on a new meaning to me, but also took on a new priority for me. At the time Sandy and I were living in an old house. We had added a bedroom onto the back, where the porch used to be. And next to that porch was a door that led underground to a small basement area that held the old boiler that heated the house. The underground space had a single light bulb hanging from the ceiling, which was actually the underside of the kitchen floor. The cement around the small area was about five feet high, and from there it was simply the dirt under the house that the home was built upon. I think the whole area must have been about a hundred square feet or less.

This area—which we used for prayer—was now accessible only through the room addition of our bedroom. We had to open the sliding closet door, move back the clothes, and open the door to the basement to get to this new prayer room. I truly was going into my closet to pray privately, as Jesus said to do in Matthew 6:6 (KJV).

Since China had such a huge impact on my heart, I had a wooden sign carved by a professional sign maker and hung it on the door. The words CHINA GAP greeted me every time I went into that dark and dingy boiler room to get away from the noise of a young, growing family and the sound of a ringing telephone. The name for my little prayer room came from the prophet Ezekiel who spoke for the Lord, saying: "So I sought for a man among them who would make a wall, and stand in the gap before Me on behalf of the land, that I should not destroy it; but I found no one" (Ezek. 22:30 NKJV).

I had purposed in my heart that I would be that man who would stand in the gap before God.

Reading this text, I saw a strong parallel to the call of Isaiah, who wrote: "Then I heard the voice of the Lord saying: 'Whom shall I send? And who will go for us?'" (Isa. 6:8). Though God could not find a man to stand in the gap during Ezekiel's ministry, he did have one who was at least willing to do so in Isaiah's ministry.

That is a good definition of intercessory prayer: to "stand in the gap" before God for others. We all know many people who are a long, long way from God. We may be the only ones anywhere near them who will pray for them. There is a distance between their lives and eternal life through Jesus Christ, and you and I can help fill that gap with prayer. Intercessory prayer allows us to plead their cause as if they were there before God's throne praying for themselves. Mr. W. J. Willis taught me how to stand in the gap.

IMAGINE THE THRILL I HAD IN SPENDING A COUPLE OF HOURS WITH BILLY GRAHAM, JUST THE TWO OF US.

Billy Graham: Pray Unceasingly

Many people in the United States would say that they know who Billy Graham is. Yet we the public don't really "know" those who are prominent among us. We "recognize them" or we "know what they stand for," but we really don't *know* them the way we know a personal friend or a family member.

So you can imagine the thrill I had in spending a couple of hours with Billy Graham, just the two of us, in a hotel room. He had graciously agreed to give me some time while he was in Sacramento, California, for a crusade in the early 1980s.

One of the things I wanted to ask him about was his prayer life. As he talked to me about his views on prayer, I listened and learned. For instance, he mentioned that while I was sitting there talking with him, he was quietly praying and asking the Lord how he could help me. He prayed for me and wanted heaven to tell him how he could guide me along my journey of service to the kingdom.

I can't tell you how many times in the past twenty years I have used that style of prayer, especially when I am talking to a young man or woman who has a burning desire to serve God. I look back and remember that Billy Graham, with all the people he knows in the world, would take time to talk with, listen to, and pray for a young man who wanted to serve God with all his heart. Another interesting insight into the prayer life of Billy Graham was the idea of "praying unceasingly," which I mentioned in a previous chapter. He told me that he prays from the moment he awakes until the moment he goes to sleep. He prays in the car, at lunch, while reading the Bible. Every situation avails itself to be prayed for, and this type of prayer can be a real motivation to "fall in love with prayer."

During the time of the apostle Paul, there was a large and populous city named Thessalonica. It was the capital of one of the four Roman districts of Macedonia. It was named after Thessalonica, the wife of Cassander, who built the city. This town is now known as Saloniki. It was in this famous city that Paul challenged the church to be alert and ready for the return of the Lord. The New Testament contains two letters written to the church in this city, which tells me that God had something important to say to the people living there.

The apostle told the people to keep communication open with heaven: "Be joyful always; pray continually; give thanks in all circumstances, for this is God's will for you in Christ Jesus. Do not put out the Spirit's fire" (1 Thess. 5:16–19).

> LIKE BILLY GRAHAM, I WILL LET EVERY SITUATION IN WHICH I FIND MYSELF BECOME AN OPPORTUNITY TO PRAY FOR SOMEONE.

The Greek word Paul chose for continually (also translated "without ceasing") literally means "without intermission." So you say, "Mike, how can I do nothing but pray all day and night? I've got to concentrate at work, and I want to be focused on my spouse and kids when I'm with them." The answer to that question is made clear in Dr. J. Vernon McGee's commentary: "This has to do with an attitude of prayer. I don't think this means that one is to stay on his knees all the time. But it means to pray regularly and to be constantly in the attitude of prayer." (McGee 1983) So by looking back in time and enjoying the legacy of prayer in my life, I have determined that, like my grandmother, I will pray to God and trust him no matter what hardships come my way. Like my mother, I will remember that all things ultimately work together for good for those who love God and are called according to his will and purpose (see Rom. 8:28).

Like Billy Graham, I will let every situation in which I find myself become an opportunity to pray for someone. And I will always keep the legacy of "praying unceasingly." If I don't see the shingles flying off the roof right away, I will still pray. I will pray looking for God to work in his timing and not mine. Like Mr. Willis, I will pray for souls, and I will pray for revival in the church. The prayers of my heart will focus on others and not on myself.

Chuck Smith: Let Your Ministry Flow from Prayer

There is not a man on the face of this tired old planet whom I respect more than my pastor, Chuck Smith. There is no way I could have received a legacy of prayer if this man had not first taught me the Bible and pointed me to God through his Word.

Chuck is lovingly known by people all around the world as "Pastor Chuck." In the thirty-three years that I have known him, I have watched him grow from the pastor of a local congregation in Costa Mesa, California, to a shepherd of a thousand churches affiliated with him around the globe. His teaching gift has drawn hundreds of thousands of people to know God and love his Word. Chuck is remembered by many as the "father of the Jesus Movement," which developed during that amazing era in the United States of the late 1960s and early 1970s when young people were searching for answers. Drugs had found their way into the mainstream of society. Millions of the *Leave it to Beaver* crowd were lost and meandering away from their loving homes and the family structure that has always been at the core of America's freedom and success.

Chuck and his wife, Kay, used to park down by the beach and pray for the hippies they saw there. As conservative as Chuck is, it was a real stretch of faith for him. But Kay had a burden for the hippies to find Jesus. I think most of the young men and women who were drawn to Chuck's teaching of the Bible at Calvary Chapel have heard this story once or twice. For many of us, it touched our hearts to think that someone from our parents' generation would actually take the time to pray for us and our generation.

Over the past thirty-three years I have been privileged to have Chuck as my mentor in the Bible and to minister at his side. Chuck's ministry to me was not only the power of God's Word, but also the importance of prayer in each believer's life. He expresses prayer in three basic forms: worship, petition, and intercession; and he believes each form of prayer has variations within it. It was by watching him that I learned the true value of prayer. The fruit of his ministry is beyond compare today, and I know that prayer is a major part of his life.

Calvary Chapel started with fifteen people being taught the Bible by Pastor Chuck. Now, thirty-five years later, there are a thousand affiliate churches; The Calvary Satellite Network broadcasting on about four hundred radio stations a day in the United States; a fifty-acre retreat center and Bible college in Southern California; a six-hundred-acre youth camp in the San Bernardino Mountains; and a twenty-five-acre retreat center, plus the main church campus of thirty acres; a Bible college in Austria in an old castle formerly used by the SS in the days of Nazi Germany; a Bible college and retreat center in Hungary; and various other fruitful ministries around the globe. From humble beginnings to far-reaching influence, we clearly see evidence of the power of prayer to expand a Spirit-filled ministry.

Chuck is a true believer in the principle "when God guides, God provides." Because of his active prayer life and dynamic faith, he has probably launched more ministries than any other person in modern church history. What is even more wonderful to me is the fact that all of Calvary Chapel's ministries are debt free. Chuck truly seeks the Lord for the provision of his work. Never have I seen him beg for money, coerce people into making donations, or make people feel guilty that they are not giving; nor have I ever seen him host a fund raiser. He prays, and God moves through his Holy Spirit acting upon God's people.

The first influence upon me from Chuck was his men's prayer meeting. It was held every Saturday night from 7:00 P.M. to 9:00 P.M. The elders of the church joined each week with Chuck to pray for the church ministry and the families of the church, and to do something I had never seen before: pray for the sick, with the laying on of hands and anointing with oil. The explosion of growth in this little country church that was built to seat 350 was a phenomenal work of God's grace and sovereignty. From the first week I gave my heart to Jesus until the time I moved to San Diego five years later, I went to every Saturday night men's prayer meeting in the little chapel that was, at the time, in the middle of Southern California bean fields.

One night I was sitting in the second row of pews with my head bowed and agreeing in prayer with all the men in the room. Every pew was filled, and people were sitting on the stage and the floors crying out to God. When Chuck called for the sick to come forward, a young man walked up and sat down in the chair at the foot of the stairs leading to the platform. He told Chuck and the elders that he had epileptic fits and that if he did not take his medicine on a daily basis, the right side of his body would go into spasms and he would have convulsions.

As I listened in awe, it immediately reminded me of one of the stories about Jesus I had read in the past month: "Some men brought to [Jesus] a paralytic, lying on a mat. When Jesus saw their faith, he said to the paralytic, 'Take heart, son; your sins are forgiven'" (Matt. 9:2). Chuck anointed the forehead of this man, and the elders gathered around to pray and lay hands on him.

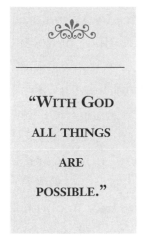

"WITH GOD ALL THINGS ARE POSSIBLE."

After a few minutes, the man stood up and proclaimed that he was healed.

At that point in my life, I was suffering from the use of drugs. (Like most people in the '60s, I actually did "inhale"!) For two years I had endured headaches, bad dreams, and hallucinations. Actually, I had thought that some people had played a dirty trick on me while attending a party. I had overdosed, and they led me to believe they were going to kill me. I left that party thinking that I had been shot in the head for some reason. It took almost two years of psychotherapy to get me to the place that I believed I was alive.

As this young man thanked Chuck, I said to myself, *I wish I could receive healing like that.* A "still, small voice" (see 1 Kings 19:12 NKJV) spoke to me and said, "Why can't you?"

I said to myself, *His problem is physical; mine is mental.*

Then I heard that voice say, "With God all things are possible."

If you don't have any background in faith or prayer, please bear with me at this point. Chuck had exercised his faith in praying for and with people. God's Holy Spirit was endorsing his faith, and it was the presence of the Holy Spirit that confirmed to me that this laying on of hands was pleasing and acceptable in the sight of the Lord.

James wrote about this practice in the New Testament: "Is anyone among you suffering? Let him pray. Is anyone cheerful? Let him sing psalms. Is anyone among you sick? Let him call for the elders of the church, and let them pray over him, anointing him with oil in the name of the Lord. And the prayer of faith will save the sick, and the Lord will raise him up. And if he has committed sins, he will be forgiven" (James 5:13–15 NKJV).

My faith was challenged, and I stepped forward to tell Chuck about my mental anguish. He reassured me that God was still on the throne and urged to trust him. As my forehead was anointed with oil, and the men laid hands on me, a peace that "passes all understanding" came upon me (see Phil. 4:7). I saw in my mind's eye an electrical charge go from the left side of my head (where I thought I had been shot) to the right side of my head. Then that "still, small voice" spoke one more time that evening: "Michael, I have not given you the spirit of fear, but of power, love, and a sound mind."

At that instant, I was healed, and my mind was back to normal. I got out of the chair and lay on the floor weeping and weeping. God had healed me and given me another chance at life.

As I began to learn the Bible, I was astounded to come upon this passage: "For God has not given us a spirit of fear, but of power and of love and of a sound mind" (2 Tim. 1:7 NKJV).

Early one Saturday morning, I went to Huntington Beach to witness about my faith and hand out Bible tracts. I went into a small coffee shop next door to a surf shop. The place held about thirty people, but it was packed with thirty-five to forty people— mostly early-morning surfers and regulars from the neighborhood. They could sit at the counter or in the worn-out red leather booths and watch the waves roll in toward the pilings on the pier and carry surfers to the shoreline.

The elderly lady who owned the shop came up to me with a pot of coffee in one hand and said, "Hey, what is it you are handing out to my customers?" I apologized if I was out of order and explained that I had accepted Jesus Christ as my Lord and Savior and wanted to give out tracts and Bibles to everyone I met. I must admit that my zeal was somewhat overwhelming for some people in my early days.

"Is that right?" she said. "Well, where do you go to church?"

I told her I attended Calvary Chapel in Costa Mesa (about ten miles from there), and proudly said that Chuck Smith was my pastor.

"Chuck Smith?" she replied. "I know Chuck Smith—known him since he was a young minister here in Huntington Beach. One Saturday night, I took my husband to him because he was an alcoholic."

She then went on to tell me the rest of the story. That particular night the prayer meeting was just ending, and people were pulling out of the parking lot. Chuck was still in the sanctuary cleaning up, so she took her husband, who was drunk at the time, and told Pastor Chuck that he had to help him. She left him in Chuck's care and drove off.

Then she said something that I thirsted to understand. She said Chuck spent the whole night with her husband and "prayed through" with him. *Prayed through*, I thought. *That is spiritual. Oh, that some day I could learn to "pray through"—whatever that means.*

Two years later, I was selected by Chuck to be an intern pastor. At one of our first weekly pastor meetings, I could not wait to ask Chuck about this lady and her husband. The minute I mentioned the coffee shop, he recalled the names of this lady and her husband. I told him of her admiration for him because he had "prayed through."

Chuck smiled and gave a soft chuckle. I did not expect what I heard next. It turns out that Chuck had tried to tell the man that Jesus could help him with his drinking problem, but the man was so drunk he could not comprehend what Chuck was saying. In fact, the man lay back on the carpet of the platform and fell asleep.

So Chuck went to his car, got a blanket out of the trunk, came back into the sanctuary, and covered the man.

Because Chuck had performed four weddings that day and led the men's prayer meeting that night, and looked forward to three morning services and one evening service the next day, he was tired. So he went home and went to bed. The man woke up in the morning and called his wife and felt great!

FALLING IN LOVE WITH PRAYER IS EASY WHEN YOU LEARN THAT PRAYER IS A GIFT FROM GOD TO YOU.

Chuck said that for years he had heard people talk about "praying through," but he didn't have a clue what it meant. Nor could he find it spoken of anywhere in the Bible. He thought it had Pentecostal origins, but had never understood it.

From that experience I learned several things. First, by watching my pastor when I was a young Christian, I learned that God likes for groups to pray together. Prayer is worship, and God uses prayer to heal people. Next, I learned that, like Chuck, I may not have all of the nomenclature down pat or know everything there is to know about prayer, but I will still pray. The "praying through" story was not anticlimactic for me after wondering what it meant for two years. In fact, it taught me that prayer is practical, and that we should be practical in our prayer life and not try to make it more than it is.

These lessons have freed me to fall in love with prayer, because I learned that it is not a task or a chore like getting up at 3:00 A.M. to milk the cows. Falling in love with prayer is easy when you learn that prayer has many aspects to it, many facets like a sparkling diamond, and that prayer is a gift from God to you.

Let me mention one more thing I have learned about prayer from my friend, mentor, and pastor. When Chuck prays in front of 10,000 people on Sunday morning or 50,000 people at a Harvest Crusade with Greg Laurie, he prays the same way as when he is standing beside a sick bed in the hospital or by the graveside at a memorial service or when he is speaking to someone on the phone: He prays in a simple, straightforward conversational tone. That knowledge freed me to realize that God hears me and wants me to talk to him the same way friends talk when they meet one another on the street.

According to the *New International Webster's Student Dictionary*, a *legacy* is: "1. Something left by will; a bequest. 2. Something handed down or derived from an ancestor or earlier time." I can vouch to you today that Ella Olson, Ruth Osborn, W. J. Willis, Billy Graham, and Chuck Smith have handed down to me a gift that gets more and more valuable with each passing day.

May I challenge you to leave a legacy of prayer for the people you love?

FALL IN LOVE WITH PRAYER
AND FALL IN LOVE WITH GOD

Now that you are at the end of this book, you may still be wondering if it is really possible for you to experience God in a new or fresh way as I have described in these pages. I want to assure you that it is not only possible, it is God's will and plan for you, and he will help you to fulfill that divine desire and destiny.

If you will allow him to do so, by the power of his Holy Spirit within you, he will cause you to fall in love with prayer. Once that happens to you, never again will you feel that you must "show up to work" or "punch a time clock" for prayer. Your prayer time will become the most important, the most productive, and (surprisingly perhaps) the most *enjoyable* time of your day.

Once you have fallen in love with prayer, it will be extremely easy and totally natural to fall in love with God himself. As you do so, your faith will become more and more contagious to your friends and family members, fellow church members, neighbors, coworkers, and acquaintances. And everything about your life will be radically changed for the better.

Then you will understand what I mean when I say that there is nothing in this world to compare with the joy that comes from *falling in love with prayer*.

READERS' GUIDE

FOR PERSONAL REFLECTION
AND GROUP DISCUSSION

BY KEITH WALL

FALLING IN LOVE WITH PRAYER

If asked to describe your prayer life in a single word, which would you choose? Exciting? Lackluster? Thrilling? Mundane?

This book began by pointing out that prayer can be—and *should* be—a grand adventure. It should fill us with a sense of awe, exhilaration, and wide-eyed anticipation. Prayer ought to permeate our lives with an edge-of-your-seat excitement to see what our invincible and unpredictable God is going to do next.

After all, prayer is the conduit that allows us to tap heaven's power source. Prayer is the honor and privilege of communicating with the Creator of the Universe. Prayer, most of all, is the means of cultivating a love relationship with our Father. What could be more awe-inspiring than that?

In the book of Acts, we read this astonishing account: "After they prayed, the place where they were meeting was shaken. And they were all filled with the Holy Spirit and spoke the word of God boldly" (4:31). Isn't that what we want our prayer life to be like? Don't we want our prayers to be filled with such vibrancy and vitality that they shake our individual lives, our communities, and our churches?

As speaker and author John Maxwell says, "The 'detonator' that churches lack today is prayer. It has the power to ignite the dynamite of the gospel and powerfully shake the world." And what's true of the church is true for individual believers. Your prayer life can be so fervent that it ignites a mighty work of the Holy Spirit.

The intent of the following study guide—indeed this entire book—is to enrich, enliven, and embolden your prayer life so that the power of God may revolutionize every aspect of your existence.

The questions that follow have been designed for use by individuals or groups. Use this guide during your personal devotions, with a prayer partner, in a Bible study group, or a Sunday school class. However you utilize this study, may you gain a fuller and deeper understanding of what it means to communicate with our almighty and loving Father.

CHAPTER ONE—THE INCREDIBLE PRIVILEGE OF PRAYER

1. The idea underlying everything in this book can be summed up in this sentence: "If you fall in love with prayer, you'll fall in love with God." Why do you think prayer is so important for cultivating a love relationship with God?

2. One of the foundational points in this chapter is that *prayer brings about spiritual awakening.* Have you had times of awakening like that—those "lightbulb" moments when you received clarity, insight, direction, or guidance—as a result of prayer?

3. Another foundational point highlighted in this chapter is that *prayer leads to spiritual growth.* Why do you think prayer and spiritual maturity are so interconnected? Is it possible for a person to grow spiritually without a strong prayer life?

4. Why do we sometimes view prayer as an obligation rather than a privilege, a duty to perform rather than a joy to experience? How can you infuse your prayer life with more delight and pleasure? In the coming weeks and months, how specifically can you grow in the area of prayer?

5. In this chapter, we learned about the great Old Testament character Enoch, who "walked with the Lord for 300 years." And we learned that the Hebrew word for *walk* means "to go on habitually." Who do you know who has walked with the Lord for a long time? What qualities and disciplines enable people to "go on habitually" in their faith year after year, decade after decade?

6. The apostle Paul wrote, "Do not be anxious about anything, but in everything, by prayer and petition, with thanksgiving, present your requests to God. And the peace of God, which transcends all understanding, will guard your hearts and your minds in Christ Jesus" (Phil. 4:6–7). Why do we sometimes fail to take all of our requests to God? Why does Paul deliberately include thanksgiving as part of his instruction? What does it mean that Jesus will "guard" our hearts and minds?

CHAPTER TWO—CONVERSING WITH THE KING

1. Since God is waiting to speak with His children at any moment, what specifically prevents you from conversing with Him more often?

2. Mike says, "We know that the King is present with us, ready and willing to converse. But it's amazing how many distractions take our focus off of Him." What distractions appear in your life to shift your focus off of the Lord?

3. This chapter contains a quote from C. S. Lewis: "We must lay before Him what is in us, not what ought to be in us." Do you ever have trouble being *completely* honest and authentic with God? What would enable you to be more open and vulnerable with Him?

4. Another quotation in this chapter came from C. H. Spurgeon, who said, "We should speak to God from our hearts and talk to Him as a child talks to his father." Do you feel that you can talk with God in this way? How did your relationship with your own dad either help or hinder the way you approach God (i.e., was he gracious or critical, tenderhearted or stern)?

5. According to Mike, "God usually will not scream and shout to get your attention. ... You may simply feel an urging, a longing, deep within you. You may feel the weight of His hand upon your shoulder." Have you ever had an experience like that? Have you felt God tugging at your heart or laying a hand on your shoulder? What were the specific circumstances?

6. The psalmist proclaimed, "How awesome is the Lord Most High, the great King over all the earth" (47:2). How does it make you feel to know you can freely approach the King of Kings? How does it change the way you view yourself to know that the Creator of the universe is eager to talk with you?

CHAPTER THREE—TO PRAY OR NOT TO PRAY?

1. With so many references to prayer in the Bible, it's obvious that this discipline is extremely important to God. Why do you think God's Word emphasizes prayer so much? What is the primary purpose of prayer in our lives?

2. In this chapter, Mike says, "God's intent for our lives is to continually shape and mold us into His image." How does God use prayer to accomplish this? In what other ways does He mold us into His image?

3. Mike shared his story of searching for God before he become a Christian and how he called out, "God, I need your help! Are you up there? Can you hear me?" Have you had a similar experience of wondering whether God was really listening to you? Think about a time God was silent even though you prayed persistently. What thoughts and feelings did those times bring up for you?

4. The New Testament writer James tells us that our requests may not be answered if we pray with selfish motives. What does this mean for the "here and now" of your life? How can we know if our motivations are pure and right?

5. Do you maintain an ongoing dialogue with God that is authentic, open, and enriching? Or does it take a desperate situation to get you to pray? If you sense the need to pray more consistently, what are some practical ways you can accomplish this?

6. Jesus said this: "I tell you the truth, my Father will give you whatever you ask in my name. Until now you have not asked for anything in my name. Ask and you will receive, and your joy will be complete" (John 16:23–24). Are you ever reluctant to ask God for something? If so, why? Why does Jesus stress the importance of asking "in my name"?

CHAPTER FOUR—THE PRIORITY OF PRAYER

1. In this chapter, Mike told how he asked Billy Graham to share his secret for developing a strong prayer life. The great evangelist gave a two-word reply: "Pray unceasingly." What exactly do you think it means to pray unceasingly? Is this something you are able to do?

2. This chapter opened with a quotation from Dwight Moody, which might be paraphrased this way: "If you're too busy to pray, then you're too busy." Do you regularly find that an overloaded schedule leaves little time for prayer? What are some specific ways you might lighten your load and free up more time for prayer?

3. Many Christians in our hectic and harried society view prayer as a task—albeit a worthwhile one—that needs to be completed and crossed off the daily to-do list. But Mike says, "We need to see prayer as the foundation, the very bedrock, of all we do." Does your prayer life reflect this principle? Do you pray about *everything* or only the *big things*? What does this say about your personal view toward prayer?

4. Mike told the story of John Wesley's mother, who was extremely busy with many children and a minister-husband. When she was exhausted and overwhelmed, she would pull her apron over her head and sit down to pray.

   When you feel burdens and stresses pressing down on you, what is your first impulse? Do you have a place to escape for prayer when you feel besieged (the park, your car, a special room)? When times get tough in your life, is prayer a *first resort* or a *last resort*?

5. People experiencing problems or crises sometimes say, "I just don't have the time to pray." To which Mike replies: "In all reality, we don't have time *not* to pray." What does this mean for your life?

6. In Mark 1:34, we read, "Very early in the morning, while it was still dark, Jesus got up, left the house and went off to a solitary place, where he prayed." Why was it necessary for Jesus to *get away* to pray? Do you have a specific time and/or place that is conducive to sustained, contemplative prayer? What can you apply from Jesus' example to your own prayer life?

CHAPTER FIVE—THE BUILDING BLOCKS OF PRAYER AND FAITH

1. Chapter five emphasizes what Mike calls building blocks—experiences, events, and people God uses to "grow us up" in the faith. What have been some of the key influences in your life to foster spiritual growth and maturity?

2. Following up on the previous question, what building blocks has God used to develop and deepen your *prayer life*?

3. Mike says, "If you will commit yourself to becoming a person of prayer, you can grow personally and you can be used to launch a new, dynamic spiritual life." What goals and dreams for the future do you have? If you were to "dream big" without limitations or restrictions, how would you like God to use you in the years to come?

4. Has God ever used you as a building block in someone else's life? In the past, what skills, talents, or qualities of yours has He used to influence others? In what ways could you better serve and encourage the people with whom you interact?

5. In this chapter, Mike shared many stories of how God answered prayer in amazing ways. Recall some of your own incredible answers to prayer. What were the specific circumstances? Has anything happened in your life that you consider "miraculous"—a clear sign of God's intervention?

6. Mike talked about Psalm 32:8, which is an important verse to him. It says in part, "I will instruct you and teach you in the way you should go. I will guide you with My eye." Can you think of some specific ways God has guided and directed your life? How does He usually guide you (through the words of other people, Scripture passages, sermons, a strong inner urging)?

CHAPTER SIX—OUR PRAYERS ON THE ALTAR

1. In chapter six, Mike describes altars as "those sacred places where sacrifices are made and meetings with the Lord take place." When you pray, do you envision yourself meeting with God someplace special and sacred? What exactly do you picture in your mind when you pray?

2. Have you had a particular request or situation that you "put on the altar"—something only God Himself could resolve? How did it turn out?

3. Mike tells us, "Abraham learned that *God's delays are not God's denials.*" Have you ever had to wait months or years to receive an answer from God? What were the specifics of that circumstance? What was it like to be in that waiting period?

4. Abraham wanted to worship the Lord on a fresh, clean altar— not on another man's altar and not on one that had been polluted by evil practices. What do you think it means to meet with God at an unsoiled, untainted altar? How can we maintain a fresh, clean altar of the heart?

5. Mike says that altars are "not only a resting place for me to catch my breath and seek God, but a resting place for prayer issues." Is it easy or difficult for you to leave prayer concerns totally in God's hands? What hinders us from trusting the Lord 100 percent with our prayer issues?

6. The apostle Paul said, "I urge you, brothers, in view of God's mercy, to offer your bodies as living sacrifices, holy and pleasing to God—this is your spiritual act of worship" (Rom. 12:1). What do you think it means to be a "living sacrifice"? And what does Paul mean when he says that being a living sacrifice is a "spiritual act of worship"?

CHAPTER SEVEN—THE POWER OF PRAYING TOGETHER

1. In this chapter, Mike says, "Somewhere between the first century and the twenty-first century, the word *church* has lost its real meaning and taken on an essence that keeps people from knowing God." Do you agree? If so, how exactly has the church lost some of its original intent and meaning?

2. Mike points out that the words "but God" appear together about fifty times in the King James Bible, signifying that God did something surprising and unexpected. Think about some of your "but God" experiences. How has God surprised you? In what ways has He done the unexpected in your life?

3. Mike tells the story of the prostitute who, as a young girl, had dreamed of becoming a nun. Her mother had said, "God wouldn't want a bad girl like you." Have you encountered individual Christians or churches that have implied (or stated outright) that God wants only *good* people? Why are churches sometimes reluctant to welcome and embrace people with a checkered past?

4. Do you currently pray with other people on a consistent basis? If so, how have you grown through the experience? If not, how might you start a prayer group or form a prayer partnership with a friend?

5. Acts 4:31 says, "And when they had prayed, the place where they were assembled together was shaken; and they were all filled with the Holy Spirit, and they spoke the word of God with boldness." Have you ever witnessed the Holy Spirit working as a direct result of your prayers? Has your church or prayer group had the sense of being filled with the Spirit?

6. In Matthew 18:20, Jesus said, "For where two or three come together in my name, there I am with them." God

certainly is with *individuals*, and He answers those who pray by themselves. So why do you think Jesus highlighted the importance of believers coming together? What do you think is God's purpose in urging people to pray as a group?

CHAPTER EIGHT—GROWING IN PRAYER

1. What person has most influenced your prayer life? How so?

2. Mike mentioned a technique he uses called "Reflex Prayer," which means praying for someone *on the spot* rather than promising to do it later (and possibly forgetting). What do you think of this approach? Why do many of us promise to pray for someone and then forget to do so? Is there a technique you have found helpful in your prayer life?

3. With what aspect of prayer do you struggle most (consistency, listening for God's voice, expressing your feelings to God, doing more than presenting a wish-list)? How you can grow in this area during the coming weeks and months?

4. In what way have you grown the most during your spiritual journey? Have you overcome—or improved on—a bad habit or a disagreeable personality trait?

5. Mike says, "We must grow beyond rote and repetitive prayers such as 'Now I lay me down to sleep' and 'Bless this food.' Our prayer life should become more and more rich, full, and joyful as we learn to talk with our heavenly Father." Why do we sometimes lapse into trite and tedious prayers? How can you keep your prayer life from becoming boring and banal?

6. James 5:16 says, "Therefore confess your sins to one another and pray for each other so that you may be healed." Why are we sometimes reluctant to "confess our sins" to our brothers and sisters in the Lord? This verse makes clear the link between prayer and healing. In what aspect of your life— physical, emotional, spiritual—do you need healing? How can you foster a spirit of openness and acceptance so others will feel free to confess their shortcomings?

CHAPTER NINE—PRAYING WITH THE RIGHT ATTITUDE

1. This chapter begins with a story about Mike's visits to Romania when that country was in the grip of corrupt leaders. He shared how humbled and inspired he was at his hosts' genuine faith and gratitude despite their desperate living conditions. Have you been around believers who exuded joy and faith in spite of difficult circumstances? How did that experience bolster your faith?

2. The United States and other western countries are blessed with affluence, material comforts, and opportunities of every kind (though there are plenty of people in these countries who struggle to make ends meet). In what ways does such prosperity hinder the Gospel from being spread? In what ways does it help? What might American Christians learn from believers in poorer countries?

3. Do you think it's wrong to pray for blessing and prosperity? Why or why not?

4. Mike makes this statement: "There are many shallow doctrines in the church today that ultimately are nothing more than distractions from the enemy. These distractions often keep people from gaining spiritual fruit from their prayers." Can you identify doctrines or beliefs popular among Christians today that ultimately undermine the truth of the gospel? How can we stand against false or misguided doctrines?

5. Mike makes the distinction between praying for *physical* blessing (a new car, a bigger house, a better job) and *spiritual* blessing (opportunities to share the Gospel, new ways to use your talents and gifts, experiences that will bring growth). In the coming weeks and months, what spiritual blessings would you like to pray for?

6. Jesus told his followers: "Watch out! Be on your guard against all kinds of greed; a man's life does not consist in the abundance of his possessions'" (Luke 12:15). What exactly did

213

Jesus mean? In what ways is our materialistic western culture at odds with Jesus' admonition? How can you apply Jesus' words to your own life?

CHAPTER TEN—PRAYER PAYS OFF PERSONALLY

1. In what ways has prayer paid off for you and your family? What prayer requests has God answered? How has your prayer life been a blessing to you and others?

2. In chapter ten Mike says, "Prayer really does pay off for us personally, but it depends largely on what payoff we're expecting." Have you ever had a prayer answered in an unexpected way? Why does God sometimes choose not to answer our prayers in the way we would like Him to?

3. Job prayed regularly on behalf of his children—that their hearts would be pure (see Job 1:4–5). Who in your circle of family members, friends, and acquaintances would you like to pray for consistently? What specifically would you pray for on behalf of this person?

4. Mike talks about praying daily for his children and future grandchild, who had not yet been born. Do you know of someone who prayed for you regularly? If so, what impact did that have on your life? How does it make you feel to know that someone was praying for you?

5. Mike quotes Psalm 119:28: "My soul melts from heaviness; strengthen me according to Your word." Then he comments, "If I were your doctor, I would give you a prescription to pray more and read more of God's Word so that you would find peace." What additional items would you include in a prescription for yourself to bring more joy and peace?

6. Jesus said, "Ask, and you will receive, that your joy may be full" (John 16:23–24). Do you think we should take this literally—that we will receive whatever we ask for—or was Jesus speaking poetically? What does the phrase "that your joy may be full" mean to you?

CHAPTER ELEVEN—THE ETERNAL VALUE OF PRAYER

1. We often become so focused on our needs right now—all of the daily nitty-gritty—that we sometimes forget about the Promised Land we're headed toward. Do you think much about heaven? Do you look forward to leaving this world and entering your heavenly home?

2. This chapter contains a quotation from Charles Spurgeon, who said, "Time is short. Eternity is long. It is only reasonable that this short life be lived in light of eternity." What changes in attitude or behavior do you need to make in order to better live in light of eternity?

3. Do you feel a clear sense of mission and purpose in life? Are you headed in a specific direction? Can you state your mission clearly and succinctly? If you're uncertain about your unique calling, how can you become more definite?

4. Toward the end of his life, Jesus told his Father in heaven, "I have brought you glory on earth by completing the work you gave me to do" (John 17:4). If you were to die right now, could you honestly say, "Yes, God, I completed my mission. I fulfilled the purpose you gave to me"? If not, what changes do you need to make in order to say that?

5. Jesus reminded us that this world, this place called earth, is not our home: "They are not of the world, even as I am not of it" (17:14). Why do we often feel rooted and attached to this world? What are some keys to developing an eternal perspective toward life and death?

6. The apostle Paul said, "For to me, to live is Christ and to die is gain. ... I desire to depart and be with Christ, which is better by far; but it is more necessary for you that I remain in the body" (Phil. 1:21, 23–24). Do you share this perspective? What will allow us to agree that "to die is gain"?

CHAPTER TWELVE — THE LEGACY OF PRAYER

1. In this chapter Mike shares stories about "prayer warriors" he has known and admired. Whom do you know who might be considered a prayer warrior? Why?

2. Mike says, "It probably would be safe to say that our love for a person can be measured by how we pray for that person." Do you agree? If so, who are the people you pray for most?

3. This chapter cites the renowned Bible teacher Dr. J. Vernon McGee, who described his idea of "praying continually" this way: "I don't think this means that one is to stay on his knees all the time. But it means to pray regularly and to be constantly in the attitude of prayer." What does it mean to be in the *attitude of prayer*? How can we develop this attitude if we don't have it already?

4. Falling in love with prayer will take away the concept that you must "show up to work" for prayer or "punch a time clock" for prayer. What can you do this week to keep your prayer life from being a chore? What creative ideas can you implement to deepen and enrich your communication with God?

5. According to Mike, a good definition for intercessory prayer is to "stand in the gap" for someone. We all know many people who are a long way from God. Who can you stand in the gap for during the coming weeks and months? What person (or people) will you commit to pray for?

6. The apostle Paul wrote, "Be joyful always; pray continually; give thanks in all circumstances, for this is God's will for you in Christ Jesus. Do not put out the Spirit's fire" (1 Thess. 5:16–19). What do you think it means to "put out the Spirit's fire"? How can we *ignite* the Spirit's fire rather than put it out?

BIBLIOGRAPHY

Easton, M.G. 1983. *The Illustrated Bible Dictionary.* Eugene, Ore.: Harvest House Publishers.

Graham, Judith. "Phone calls to God are bedeviling." *Chicago Tribune*, 29 May 2003.

Guest, John and R.C. Sproul, Jr. 1992. *Finding Deeper Intimacy with God: Only a Prayer Away.* Grand Rapids, Mich.: Baker Book House.

Mann, Chester, and Dwight Lyman Moody. 1997. *D. L. Moody—Soul Winner.* Greenville, S.C.: Ambassador-Emerald Int.

Manning, Brennan. 2003. *A Glimpse of Jesus.* San Francisco: HarperSanFrancisco.

McGee, J. Vernon. 1983. *Thru the Bible.* Nashville: Thomas Nelson.

Miller, Basil. 1941. *George Muller, Man of Faith and Miracles.* Minneapolis, Minn.: Bethany House Publishers.

Orr, James, M.A., D.D., gen. ed. 1988. *International Standard Bible Encyclopedia.* Grand Rapids, Mich.: Wm. B. Eerdmans Publishing Company.

Sayers, Dorothy L. "Dorothy L. Sayers: Her Life and Soul." *Christianity Today* vol. 41 no. 11 (1998).

Strong, James. 1997. *The New Strong's Exhaustive Concordance of the Bible.* Nashville: Thomas Nelson.

Swindoll, Charles. 1998. *Strengthening Your Grip.* Waco, Tex.: Word Publishing Group.

Vine, W. E. 1996. *Vine's Complete Expository Dictionary of Old and New Testament Words.* Nashville: Thomas Nelson, Inc.

Also available...

FALLING IN LOVE
WITH THE BIBLE

The second in Mike MacIntosh's inspiring series—designed to help today's reader re-embrace the essential basics of the Christian life.

The Word at Work Around the World

A vital part of Cook Communications Ministries is our international outreach, Cook Communications Ministries International (CCMI). Your purchase of this book, and of other books and Christian-growth products from Cook, enables CCMI to provide Bibles and Christian literature to people in more than 150 languages in 65 countries.

Cook Communications Ministries is a not-for-profit, self-supporting organization. Revenues from sales of our books, Bible curricula, and other church and home products not only fund our U.S. ministry, but also fund our CCMI ministry around the world. One hundred percent of donations to CCMI go to our international literature programs.

CCMI reaches out internationally in three ways:

• Our premier International Christian Publishing Institute (ICPI) trains leaders from nationally led publishing houses around the world.

• We provide literature for pastors, evangelists, and Christian workers in their national language.

• We reach people at risk—refugees, AIDS victims, street children, and famine victims—with God's Word.

Word Power, God's Power

Faith Kidz, RiverOak, Honor, Life Journey, Victor, NexGen — every time you purchase a book produced by Cook Communications Ministries, you not only meet a vital personal need in your life or in the life of someone you love, but you're also a part of ministering to José in Colombia, Humberto in Chile, Gousa in India, or Lidiane in Brazil. You help make it possible for a pastor in China, a child in Peru, or a mother in West Africa to enjoy a life-changing book. And because you helped, children and adults around the world are learning God's Word and walking in his ways.

Thank you for your partnership in helping to disciple the world. May God bless you with the power of his Word in your life.

For more information about our international ministries, visit www.ccmi.org.

Additional copies of *FALLING IN LOVE WITH PRAYER*
are available from your local bookseller.

If you have enjoyed this book,
or if it has had an impact on your life,
we would like to hear from you.

Please contact us at:

VICTOR BOOKS
Cook Communications Ministries, Dept. 201
4050 Lee Vance View
Colorado Springs, CO 80918

Or visit our Web site: www.cookministries.com

Victor®
The Bible Teacher's Teacher